PRAISE FOR
SPEAK WITH IMPACT

"Allison Shapira has become not only a master of public speaking but one of the best speech coaches in the US. In this new book, she provides a clear, practical roadmap for those who want to have an impact in today's clamorous world. If you want to excel on your feet, read this, keep this, and read again."

—**DAVID GERGEN,**
CNN senior political analyst,
Harvard Kennedy School professor of public service,
and former White House advisor to four presidents

"Allison can prove and has proven that anyone can learn to lead; it all starts with your voice."

—**JORDAN HEWSON,**
founder, Speakable

"If you want to improve your public speaking, spend a few hours with Allison's book. It's loaded with good advice and tricks of the trade that will help you up your game."

—**DAN HEATH,**
coauthor of *Made to Stick* and *The Power of Moments*

"The brilliance of *Speak with Impact* is in its simple genius. Allison's lessons are by nature specific, practical, and transferable. With Allison's help, I was able to arm my team with the proper tools needed to enhance their presentations skills and build self-assurance in public speaking."

—**DEBORAH DUGAN,**
CEO, (RED)

"Allison has written a practical and thoughtful guide to public speaking that equips the reader with a powerful set of tools that are applicable to any presentation or speaking opportunity. Allison successfully blends her narrative voice with key takeaways that I found to be incredibly useful."

—**BRUCE SOLL,**
senior VP and counsel of company affairs, L Brands

"Allison Shapira's new book is as much about leadership as it is about public speaking. She prods us to ask tough questions: what do we want to accomplish, who is our audience, why should they listen to us? And then she makes us critique ourselves and test our messages with the audience. I wish I had met her years ago."

—**GERALDINE LAYBOURNE,**
media entrepreneur, first president, Nickelodeon, cofounder, Oxygen

"Reading *Speak with Impact* is like having a one-on-one session with a master trainer in public speaking. Allison Shapira's practical advice and well-hewn insights are captured on every page and will give novice speakers confidence and seasoned veterans a stronger voice."

—JEFFREY SEGLIN,
director and senior lecturer, Harvard
Kennedy School Communications Program

"Allison skillfully commands the attention of her audiences with professionalism, grace, humor, and insight. Through *Speak with Impact*, she provides pragmatic tools, practical advice, and examples that will help readers build powerful public speaking skills."

—ZOË DEAN-SMITH,
vice president, economic empowerment &
entrepreneurship, Vital Voices Global Partnership

SPEAK WITH
IMPACT

How to Command the Room and Influence Others

ALLISON SHAPIRA

HARPERCOLLINS
LEADERSHIP

AN IMPRINT OF HARPERCOLLINS

Published by HarperCollins Leadership, an imprint of HarperCollins.

Book design by Elyse Strongin, Neuwirth & Associates.

978-0-8144-3936-4 (eBook)

Library of Congress Control Number: 2018956212

978-0-8144-3971-5

Printed in the United States of America
19 20 21 22 LSC 10 9 8 7 6 5 4 3

Contents

Acknowledgments

The act of writing may be a solitary process, but publishing a book takes a team. From conducting research to sharing advice to providing feedback, a significant number of people can be seen, felt, and heard in this book.

Thank you to Anthony Mattero at CAA, whose expert advice guided me throughout the process, and to Ellen Kadin, who recognized the need for this book and took a chance on a new author. Thank you to Jeff Farr at Neuwirth & Associates and Timothy Burgard and the team at HarperCollins Leadership for their partnership and enthusiastic support.

Friends and fellow authors Diane Mulcahy and Jennefer Witter readied me for the writing process and continue to model the way. Emily Adams sifted through pages of dense academic papers and left no digital stone unturned to verify a statistic or simplify a concept. Jeffrey Seglin was a constant source of wisdom and patience through my countless questions. David Gergen's mentorship paved the way for many of the experiences in this book. Arthur and Barbara Bushkin have been incredible champions of both the book and my career.

Friends, colleagues, and mentors spent hours reading and reviewing the manuscript and gave me honest and practical feedback: Paul Anghinetti, Margaux Bergen, Trudi Bresner, Marie Danziger, Timothy Patrick McCarthy, and Jeanine Turner.

Dozens of people agreed to be interviewed or quoted, many of whom are friends or colleagues and a few of whom have never met me: Sidd Chopra, Roger Courville, Jacki Coyle, Glenn Croston, Marshall Ganz, Hadas Golan, Kristi Hedges, Stephen Krupin, Timothy Moffett, Helen Moses, Tim Murphey, Scott Perlo, Mike Rayburn, Matthew Rees, Tamara Elliott Rogers, Olivia Schofield, Annette Simmons, Patrick Pendleton Smith, Bruce Turkel, David Wells, and Gordon Whitman.

Many others provided invaluable support along this journey: Morra Aarons-Mele, Sedrick Banks, Kimberly Berger, Bill Cates, Barbara Day, Zoë Dean-Smith, Greg Dinkin, Deborah Dugan, Rob Eager, Gregg Gregory, Dan Heath, Jordan Hewson, Sabra Horne, Dara Iserson, Jinnyn Jacob, Marcus Johnson, Geraldine Laybourne, Brian Mandell, Raegan Moya-Jones, Arnold Sanow, and Bruce Soll.

To the stellar team at Global Public Speaking, especially Meghan Gonzalez and Brittan Stockert: thank you for making the business run so smoothly while I was sequestered throughout the writing process.

To my parents, Betty and Richard Greenspan, and my brothers, Shaun, Peter, and Scott: thank you for trusting me six years ago when I took an enormous leap of faith.

To the thousands of women and men whom I've worked with over the past fifteen years, thank you for confiding in me your challenges and goals, your fears and insecurities, your hopes and aspirations. Your willingness to be vulnerable showed me how similar we all are, and your experiences turned into powerful teaching lessons that will empower people around the world.

Introduction

Confessions of a Former Opera Singer

It was 1996. I was an undergraduate music student at Boston University. A younger, eager sophomore in the vocal performance program, I was about to have a difficult conversation with my voice teacher. I just didn't know it yet.

We were in her office during one of our weekly voice lessons: she was sitting at her baby grand piano, one hand resting on the keys, one hand flipping absentmindedly through *People* magazine, as she sometimes did during our lessons. I was standing a few feet away, in the curve of the piano's body, waiting for her to play a scale.

After she finished playing one of those scales, in the middle of the lesson, my voice teacher casually said something that made my heart drop to the floor. She said, "You know, you might want to consider other avenues for a musical career besides performing."

I had wanted to be an opera singer since I was thirteen years old. I had studied in the Visual and Performing Arts program at Booker High School in Sarasota, Florida, and had spent my teenage years as an overachieving young vocalist: competing, singing, studying, performing. I had trained in the Tanglewood Young Artists Vocal Program in Lenox, Massachusetts, and I was about to spend my upcoming summer in Italy with the prestigious Curtis Institute of Music.

Now here I was, an aspiring opera singer at Boston University, with my mentor and teacher—one of the most influential people in my life—telling me I wasn't good enough to make it in the industry.

To tell you the truth, a part of me had known it was coming. I had spent my whole life focused on performing. But when I arrived at college, something had happened: I started to lose my passion for singing. My music teachers said I became "distracted" by subjects like international relations, astrophysics, and foreign languages. Day after day, I felt confined to an underground practice room the size of a closet, playing the piano or singing while dreaming of traveling around the world. My mind was anywhere but in that tiny room; singing had become a chore.

When my voice teacher suggested that I wasn't good enough to be an opera singer, yes, I was devastated—but I was also set free. Liberated from the strict bonds of classical music, I could choose to be anything in life. The problem was, I had no idea what to choose. I changed majors and stopped singing for over a decade. It would take me that long to find my voice.

From Singing to Speaking

I graduated from college with a major in Italian Language and Literature. "What a practical degree," I remember my father remarking dryly but lovingly. At the time, I never thought that I would use my vocal training again. I thought it would be relegated to a "fun fact" during corporate icebreakers, or my secret weapon at karaoke. I soon realized I was wrong.

One of my first jobs after college was at the Consulate General of Israel in Boston. I was a local American employee working on the public affairs team of a foreign government. I soon found out that I would have to give speeches—and speak on behalf of a foreign government during a very turbulent time in the Middle East.

I was terrified. I had never given a speech in my life—or, to be more correct, my first and last speech had been during my Bat Mitzvah, around the same time I started singing.

It was a surprising contrast: I could confidently don a green, gem-studded ball gown and stand in front of two thousand people performing a Mozart aria. But the thought of standing onstage in a business suit, with no background music, performing something *I had written*, filled me with fear.

Asking around, I found out about Toastmasters International, a global organization whose members come together to practice their public speaking and leadership skills in a safe, comfortable environment.[1] I joined the Boston Toastmasters Club and started attending bimonthly meetings. As I learned certain techniques of public speaking—eye contact, body language, and vocal variety—I realized that *I already had these skills*. Because of my operatic training, I knew how to feel comfortable onstage. I knew how to create an emotional connection with my audience. I knew how to use my voice to project power, confidence, and authority. I had stage presence: I simply had to convert it into executive presence.

Perhaps most importantly, I knew how to coach others. As aspiring opera singers, we spend much of our time coaching one another on pronunciation, posture, and breathing. Through years of training, I had developed a very critical eye and ear for observing others and a very diplomatic way of giving feedback. I knew how to listen patiently with laser-sharp focus and pick up on subtle vocal shifts and body movements that either enhanced or detracted from a performance.

There were of course major differences between speaking and singing. When I sang, I was performing other people's music: Mozart, Puccini, and Schubert. There was background music to keep me on track and a conductor interpreting the composer's message.

At the Israeli Consulate, I now needed to write and deliver my own speeches and then take public responsibility for those messages. And do it on behalf of a foreign government. In a time of conflict in the Middle East. At age twenty-three. I had never before worked in international relations and was unprepared for the visceral responses—both positive and negative—to my speeches. I was nervous before every speech and prepared for the worst.

I had to learn speechwriting tools such as messaging, structure, and persuasion. I needed to prepare for difficult questions from a hostile audience. I may have been a "natural" on delivery, but I needed to overcome the steep learning curve of content creation.

Through Toastmasters and on-the-job trial and error (a lot of error), my speaking rapidly improved. Soon, I was writing the diplomats' speeches and coaching them on their public speaking skills. When a last-minute emergency prevented them from giving a speech, I'd give the speech in their place. I became the president of the Boston Toastmasters Club.

One day, I received an email that would change the trajectory of my professional career. A woman reached out and said that her boss—a doctor who headed up a local nonprofit organization—had an important presentation coming up.

She asked, "Could Toastmasters help him?"

I replied, "Of course!" and I encouraged her boss to join the club, come to meetings, and give speeches every month. "Over time," I said cheerily, "he will make great improvements!"

She responded, "No, you don't understand. His speech is on Tuesday. Do you know anyone who can come to his office and help him prepare?"

I thought about it for a minute and then replied, "Well, for a small hourly fee, I guess I could come to your boss's office and help him prepare. But it wouldn't be through Toastmasters."

A week later, holding my very first coaching check, I had a major realization as an entrepreneur: *I had very valuable knowledge that others would pay to learn.* That night, I ordered business cards. I would slowly build that business over the next fifteen years.

Finding My Voice

For over a decade, singing did in fact become my fun fact during icebreakers and my secret weapon at karaoke. I even sang the National Anthem for the Boston Red Sox at Fenway Park in 2004. But I wanted to do more.

I missed singing and missed performing. What I really wanted to sing, however, wasn't opera—it was the folk revival music of the 1960s that my parents had listened to when I was growing up: Joan Baez, Bob Dylan, and Judy Collins. When I let loose, I sang folk music.

So in 2011, soon after graduating from the Harvard Kennedy School with a master of public administration, I started to sing folk songs at open mic nights around Boston and Cambridge, Massachusetts. I borrowed a guitar from a friend and took lessons online to accompany myself.

Putting together voice and guitar turned into a magical combination: suddenly I could play and sing nearly any song in the world. And I was set free.

Folk music wasn't the structured, perfectionist opera that everyone else thought I should sing, where you were under the direction of the conductor or beholden to the composer, where you were evaluated on the perfect pitch of a single tone or the proper pronunciation of an Italian vowel.

In folk music, I could sing any song I wanted, I could play it any way I wanted, and *I didn't need to be perfect*. Nobody cared if I dropped a consonant here or there; in fact, folk audiences were impressed that they could understand the words at all. What they demanded was authenticity, not perfection. I felt empowered and inspired. Liberated from the bonds of opera, I started to write my own songs. One year after learning to play the guitar, I released an album of original music. I had found my voice.

Helping Others Find Their Voice

What I thought would be an interesting side career in folk music actually had a pivotal effect on my public speaking business. Once I found my own voice, I wanted to help others find their voice when they spoke in public. Instead of creating a false speaker persona based on who they thought they should be, I wanted to help people connect with their natural drive, and then harness that drive to speak with power and authenticity. I knew that's how they would make an impact on others.

In 2012, I took a leap of faith. After ten years of teaching public speaking on the side, I decided to move from Boston to Washington, DC, and launch the business full-time. I moved to DC without a single client but with a supportive network of friends, former classmates, and colleagues. Within the first year, I had over thirty clients. The business grew so quickly that I hired a team of coaches and trainers so we could help even more people.

Over the years, I've had incredible opportunities to teach public speaking and presentation skills: at the Harvard Kennedy School and Georgetown University, for the United States government and foreign governments, and for global Fortune 500 companies. I've had the honor of working with the nonprofit organization Vital Voices Global Partnership, traveling around the world building communication skills in women leaders who are growing a business, running for office, or launching a nonprofit.

I've worked with groups and individuals on-site in Africa, Europe, Asia, South America, and the Middle East, and taught classes with twenty different nationalities in one room. I've witnessed people from every region in the world all fight through the exact same fears: fear of being in front of an audience, fear of forgetting their message, and fear of being inadequate. Similarly, I've heard them express the very same desires: the desire to stand confidently in front of an audience, the desire to speak from the heart, and the desire to move people to action. And while I've seen that the contexts differ widely from country to country, the process of preparing to speak in public is the same. Your tone of voice may change in different languages, your hand gestures might be driven by your audience's culture, but we all need to take time to prepare and practice. Across all industries and sectors, across all levels of experience, there is an insatiable need for public speaking skills. We feel the need to connect with others because connection is what makes us feel human.

Nearly every person I worked with had a hunger for authenticity and self-actualization. While I coached people in public speaking, I wasn't just teaching them how to write a concise speech or use effective body language. Coaching and training became a way for people to find out who they really are, why they are called to speak, and how they can have an impact on the world around them. So many people have something to say but lack the skills or the courage to say it. Public speaking, then, is about more than just skill-building; it's a critical part of leadership development.

As people move into more senior leadership positions, they spend more time communicating with others: empowering, motivating, negotiating, and serving as a role model. In their communities and in the world at large, they're faced with pressing social, environmental, economic, and political challenges. As we face a growing number of crises in the world around us, we invariably think, "What can I do to make an impact?" If leadership is about bringing people together to achieve a common goal, then we can lead at work, in our communities, or on the global stage. It starts with speaking up.

Speak with Impact: How to Command the Room and Influence Others gives you the tools to build your confidence and find your voice. It includes strategies, stories, and exercises that walk you through the process of writing, practicing, and delivering a speech or presentation or holding an important conversation. It reveals some of the most innovative solutions from the fields of music, academia, and international business. It contains practical and immediately applicable steps that busy professionals can use to improve their speaking skills amidst a day full of competing priorities, with tools and tips to maximize their time and create a powerful, impactful message that inspires their audiences to action.

From "How to write a speech in thirty minutes" to a more detailed process for some of the most important speeches of your professional career, this book calls on my experience working with men and women at all stages of their life, in dozens of countries and industries around the world. I'm not the only source of knowledge in this book: I bring in the opinions of other experts in the field of public speaking and beyond and share the many lessons I've learned from my students. I also share what my team and I have learned from our clients, and you'll hear me use the pronoun "we" when including the other talented trainers and coaches at Global Public Speaking.

This book will also help you build executive presence, which can either hold you back in your career or catapult you to the top of your organization. Regardless of your job, age, or years of experience, your abilities to speak well under pressure and build trusting relationships with those around you are critical components of your leadership effectiveness in any setting.

In the first half of the book, I provide a path for you to connect with your drive to speak and draft content that is authentic and genuine. I walk you through a process for writing, polishing, and practicing your content. I provide tools for engaging with your audience and ensuring that your nonverbal delivery matches your words. I teach you the breathing techniques of opera singers to calm your nerves and strengthen your voice. In the second half of the book, I discuss different types of speaking situations that you might face, from panels to conference calls, and provide specific techniques for mastering those situations. I end with a call to action for how to use these skills going forward.

I've also added additional resources to my website. Throughout the book, the ⊕ icon indicates more information, resources, and videos at www.speakwithimpactbook.com, and the ▓ icon indicates which exercises you can come back to for practice.

Keep this book on your desk or in your home and refer to it when you want to use your voice to have an impact on the world around you. Whether you have a presentation in your first job out of college or you're addressing the entire company in your new role as CEO, this book will guide you through the process.

Public speaking is not about getting up and reading a script. It's about looking deep into yourself to ask what you want to say and who needs to hear it. Then it's about building your confidence and your skills to speak with power, ability, and authenticity. Finally, it's about taking action based on your ideas.

Public speaking is exercising leadership with your voice—speaking up on behalf of your ideas, your vision, your organization, or your community—and persuading others to join you to achieve a shared goal.

No matter where you live, what you do, or what stage you are at in your career, *you have something powerful to say, and you have a right to say it.*

When we connect with what truly drives us, when we find the courage to speak up, and when we act on our words, we have a positive and powerful impact on the world around us.

CHAPTER 1

Before You Speak

What Is Public Speaking,
and Where Does It Happen?

USING THIS BOOK

This book is designed to walk you through the process of writing, practicing, and delivering a speech or presentation in front of any audience. The first half outlines the process I've developed over the past fifteen years. The second half prepares you for different speaking situations, from moderating a panel to speaking off the cuff.

Identify an upcoming speaking opportunity and use this book to prepare. If you don't have one coming up, the section "Finding opportunities to speak" will help you.

Find a practice partner with whom you can practice what you learn in this book. It should be someone you trust who can give you genuine feedback: a friend, family member, or colleague. Talk through your goals and fears about public speaking with this person, and practice your speech drafts along the way. Because public speaking revolves around the impact we have on others when we speak, it's important to practice your speech with others to ensure that you are having the intended impact.

Alternately, you could form a book club and go through this book as a community. Before each meeting, read a chapter of the book and then come together to practice what you learn and apply it to your upcoming speech. Celebrate your progress and successes together.

Use this book as a practical, skill-building manual. Write in it, highlight it, and dog-ear the pages or take notes on your digital copy. It's intended to help you again and again. Many sections end with an exercise to apply directly to your speech or presentation. Each time you have an upcoming speech, you can quickly go through the exercises to prepare.

Don't try to go through this book all in one sitting. As you'll learn in Chapter 3, writing is an interactive process. Spend some time reading and writing, then take a break. You'll learn about the power of "Pause and Breathe" in Chapter 7; beyond being a practical technique to avoid filler words and give your audience time to absorb your message, *pause and breathe* is a philosophy for calming your nerves and living your life.

VISUALIZING YOUR GOAL

If you're listening to this book as an audiobook, close your eyes and listen to this paragraph. If you're reading it, then as soon as you finish this paragraph, close your eyes and visualize it: *You are about to give a speech. You're nervous, but you feel excited and ready. You walk onstage with confidence and a sense of purpose. You make eye contact with your audience, pause and breathe, and then deliver an opening sentence that captures people's attention. You describe a central, compelling message that resonates with the audience and causes them to think differently about the world. You can see heads nodding and some people taking notes. You speak in a genuine, warm tone that makes people feel like you are having a conversation with them, like you would be the same person onstage as offstage. You use personal examples that illustrate your main message and include a call to action that underscores the urgency of your message. You finish to strong applause and a feeling of excitement and accomplishment. You did it!*

How do you feel? I imagine if the above happened to you, you would feel energized, excited, and purposeful. That's exactly how I'd like you to feel, whether you are walking out onstage or striding confidently into a conference room. That's why I've written this book.

DEFINING PUBLIC SPEAKING

What's the difference between public speaking and presentation skills?

"I don't speak in public, but I give presentations every day."

I remember the quizzical look I gave the woman who said that to me many years ago. I realized we might have different definitions of the same concept.

Close your eyes and picture someone who is "public speaking." Where are they? What are they doing? Chances are, you picture someone standing on a podium, looking out at a vast crowd. You can hear a pin drop in the audience as she clears her throat and prepares to speak. Maybe she has a script, and maybe she uses a microphone. There's nothing casual about it; it's a formal speech.

A formal speech is certainly one example of public speaking. Giving a presentation is another example, when you convey information to an audience. You are probably in a smaller setting like a conference room, you might use visual aids or handouts, and your focus is more informational than inspirational. There is also some overlap between the two types of speaking. A presentation can be inspiring. A speech can be informative. Every time you communicate, you have an opportunity to influence others and make an impact.

I believe public speaking happens *any time you speak with an audience of one or more people with some purpose*. It's something you do every single day, at work and at home. It's a speech, presentation, or conversation, and it can happen in person, by phone, or by video. Why use such a broad definition? Because if we define public speaking as standing up and making formal remarks to an attentive audience, then we'll be neglecting the daily opportunities we have to connect with, influence, and inspire others.

Take a minute and think about what kind of speaking you do, with an audience of one or more, with some goal: You're being interviewed for your dream job or pitching a client, prospect, investor, or donor. You're having a difficult conversation with a direct report or addressing the entire company across different time zones. You're speaking up on a conference call or leading a video webinar. You're running for political office or trying to bring together your community to take action. You're speaking at a conference or walking into a networking event. In each and every one of these situations, you are speaking with an audience of one or more with some purpose. You are speaking in public, and you have an opportunity to make an impact.

Ever since the day that woman told me, "I don't speak in public, but I give presentations every day," I have used both phrases together. Not because *I* believe they are separate, but because *you* might believe they are separate. And one of the first lessons in public speaking is to know your audience and their assumptions. If you relate to the phrase "presentation skills," then that's what I will use to get your attention instead of trying to convince you that my phrase is more inclusive. This book will cover all of it.

We Do This All Around the World

No matter what country we live in, what language we speak, what industry we work in, or what stage we are at in our career, every single one of us speaks in public. Public speaking is one of the most powerful and ancient ways in which we connect with others.

I've worked with Armenian economists, British investment bankers, Israeli diplomats, Japanese entrepreneurs, Palestinian investors, and women business owners from Argentina to Rwanda to Afghanistan. In this book, we'll talk about what is universal in public speaking and what is culturally specific so that you can give a powerful speech in English, Arabic, Spanish, or Kinyarwanda.

Is It Talking *At* People, or Talking *With* Them?

Many people don't like public speaking because they hate to be the center of attention, or perhaps because they don't like lecturing other people. Here is some good news: it's not about making you the center of attention. A powerful speech should feel like a conversation between you and every single person in the audience, no matter the size.

As we'll discuss later on, when you focus on the message instead of the messenger, then many of your nerves dissipate. You no longer become the center of attention: *your idea* becomes the center of attention, and *your audience* becomes the focus.

Is Public Speaking a Skill or a Talent?

Many people use the excuse that public speaking is a talent that they weren't born with. My experience and the experience of my clients has taught me that *public speaking is a skill*. In fact, it's a core belief upon which I built my company. While some people may be naturally better than others, it's something that every single person can learn through practice and feedback. It's a skill that you can learn and master. It's a skill that this book will help you build.

Is Public Speaking About Substance, or Style?

Public speaking is not about dressing up a boring message with jazzy hand gestures or a charming smile. It's first and foremost about crafting a compelling message that resonates with you and your audience. Then it's about delivering that message in a way that engages your audience's attention by using body language and eye contact that enhance instead of distract from the speech. It's about *both* substance and style, content and delivery.

Imagine a speaker with all substance and no style. She knows everything there is to know about her subject and has crafted a beautiful speech. However, she buries her nose in her notes, reads word-for-word from the page, and speaks in a flat, lifeless voice. Will she capture your attention? Will you listen to her entire message? Or will your mind wander to the things you didn't get done at work that day or what time you have to pick up your kids from school?

Now imagine a speaker with all style and no substance. He smiles widely at the audience, moves masterfully around the stage, and speaks with a warm, booming voice. He makes meaningful eye contact and pauses to make sure you've absorbed the message. The problem is, there is no message—he speaks in platitudes we've all heard before and doesn't have a compelling point. In fact, you're wondering what the message is at all. There's a humorous example of this at www. speakwithimpactbook.com. ⊕

Whether in a conference room or onstage, when you combine a powerful message with engaging and authentic delivery, you capture people's attention and compel them to listen. You connect with them on a personal level, which lets them see you as a human being. This builds trust with the audience because it demonstrates how much you have in common. When you do this, your words have maximum impact.

Some people will discredit the importance of nonverbal communication. Some experts will tell you that it's all about the strength of their argument and the veracity of their data. I disagree. Professor Alex "Sandy" Pentland of MIT's Human Dynamics Laboratory explains that nonverbal signals predate human language. We pick up on these "honest signals" far more quickly than we do the language itself. So while we may think it's just about the content, we're reading cues before the speaker even says a word.[1]

Why Is Public Speaking Important?

If you've purchased this book, then you already have some idea of why public speaking is important. Maybe you're still scarred from that first public speaking experience you had in middle school, or maybe it happened last week at a staff meeting, or you have just been informed that you will have to give a toast at your best friend's wedding.

Why go through all the effort to learn how to speak in public? Isn't it easier just to hide behind email or strategically delegate the presentation to someone else?

Speech is one of the most powerful tools we have as human beings. It's one of the ways in which we build trust with others: if you want to get to know someone, you talk to them. In studying high-performing teams, Professor Pentland found face-to-face communication to be the most valuable form of communication.[2] Regardless of all the digital ways we can connect, there is no form of communication as powerful as an in-person conversation—to clear up a controversy, inform people of a new procedure, or inspire a community to take action. There's an energy in the room, an electricity, a bond that's formed when a group of people sits together in the same space and goes through the same experience. When you *lead* that experience, you connect with people on a new level.

This book will help you build trust with clients and prospects and move up within your career. It will help you manage difficult conversations and lead a team or an organization. It will help you build confidence in yourself and help you connect with others on a deeply personal level. It will help you pass your knowledge on to the next generation and become an advocate on behalf of what you believe in.

FINDING OPPORTUNITIES TO SPEAK

We have daily opportunities to practice public speaking. If you're more junior in your career, speaking up is how you build your visibility and reputation within the organization. If you're a senior executive who is used to strategically delegating a presentation to others due to your own fear, the opportunities below give you ways to take back those speaking roles.

Professional Opportunities

Speak up in a meeting: The easiest and quickest way to speak in public is to *speak up* in a meeting or on a conference call. One senior banking executive I worked with said to me that, early in her career, she went to every single meeting ready to make a point. She prepared bullet points in advance so that when she spoke, seemingly off the cuff, she would feel and sound confident. That banking executive is now a model public speaker for her organization.

Again and again, when managers send their direct reports through our training programs, they will say to me, "Look, if they're in the room for a meeting, we expect them to speak up. Don't just sit there in silence." Recognize that if you are in the room, you may be expected to contribute.

What if someone else makes your point before you do? In that case, you can simply refer to that person's point and build on it. I call this "compliment and build," and it's a useful tactic for interrupting someone long-winded. Wait for that person to take a breath and then jump in to compliment him, build on his point, and take the conversation in a new direction.

Volunteer to present at a meeting: No matter what industry you work in, meetings provide opportunities for people to present information to one another. Depending on your work culture, it's either *easier* or *harder* to speak in front of colleagues. A lot of professionals will say, "I have no problem speaking to clients; I built my career doing that. But I'm terrified of speaking in front of internal leaders." However, the leaders of that same organization will say to us, "Did you hear how nervously he presented in the last meeting? Does he speak to our *clients* like that?"

No matter who is in the meeting, presenting is a terrific opportunity to build and demonstrate your knowledge. If you're more junior in your career, let your manager know that you

would like to present at an upcoming meeting. If you're a mid-
to senior-level manager or executive, you have an opportunity
to model for your subordinates the behavior you expect. By
speaking in these meetings, you are setting the tone and conveying the message you'd like them to convey to others.

Volunteer to speak at a community event: Many companies
we work with encourage their employees to participate in
community organizations on behalf of the company. It's a
great way for those employees to promote a good cause while
also increasing goodwill toward their company. Speaking to
that community group on behalf of your organization gives
you an opportunity to talk about something you truly believe
in, while also finding a way to put a human face to your
company.

Speak at a conference: Whatever your field, from neurosci-
ence to supply-chain logistics, speaking at a conference is a
powerful way to elevate your own professional brand and also
represent your company. You don't have to be the keynote
speaker! You can sit on a panel or lead a breakout session.

Speak up at a conference: Come prepared to ask questions
during a conference. It's a great opportunity to practice your
speaking skills and also build your visibility. Prepare a few questions based on the speaker or the subject, and choose one according to how the presentation goes. Someone could come up
to you afterward and say, "I thought that was a great question.
Can I speak more with you about this?" Or, better yet, "Can I
hire you to help my company through the same challenge?"

Lead a webinar: When your company doesn't have a budget
for travel, leading a webinar can be a great way to practice public speaking skills. Offer to discuss a recent project or a new development in your field.

Speak to clients: If your role is more internal in an organization, look for opportunities to move into a client-facing role.
Can you join your colleagues when calling on clients? Can you
incorporate more business development into your role, where
you leave the office and attend events? Your meetings with
clients or prospects provide terrific opportunities to speak in
public.

Attend networking events: One of the easiest and most low-
risk speaking opportunities is to attend networking events outside of work. Introducing yourself to others and talking about
what you do is a great way to practice your public speaking
skills. These events are also a terrific way to practice another
very important speaking skill: listening. Many people hate networking events because they think of pushy salespeople selling
something, or lobbyists promoting an agenda. However, networking events provide a great opportunity to get to know other
people and be inquisitive about what they do.

Professional associations: What membership associations
do you belong to? Those organizations plan the regional and
national conferences we spoke about above. When you take on
a leadership role within those organizations, serving on the
board or chairing a committee, you find opportunities to speak
by moderating a panel or introducing a speaker. If you're just
starting out in your career, these associations provide terrific
ways to build your network and connect with others in your
field.

Personal Opportunities

Outside of work, there are just as many opportunities to speak in
public.

In politics: If you're unhappy with the direction your neighborhood is going or the course your country is taking, get involved in politics and run for office. Not only are you actively taking responsibilities for your community, you will find endless opportunities to speak in public.

In your religious community: Offer to lead sermons or read a portion of the holy text at your prayer service. This can be a meaningful way to practice your skills and also connect with your spirituality.

In your alumni group: No matter where you went to school, your *alma mater* probably has an alumni association that holds events. Join the alumni association or attend meetings, and you will find opportunities to speak at events.

When I first moved to Washington, DC, I joined the Harvard Kennedy School DC Alumni Council and spent two years as its president. I gave opening remarks at every single event we held, from an informal breakfast at the National Press Club to a high-profile panel at the National Archives. It was an incredibly effective way to build my profile in Washington, practice my skills, and create long-lasting relationships with friends, colleagues, and prospective clients.

In your issue area: Do you have a child with special needs or do you come from an underrepresented community? Are you a lifelong member of an advocacy organization? Joining or leading an organization that represents those issues gives you opportunities to speak up and contribute to something you believe in.

Join Toastmasters:[3] Founded in 1924, Toastmasters International remains one of the best ways to practice your public speaking skills.[4] During regular meetings held around the globe, Toastmasters provides a safe space for practice and feedback in a comfortable, supportive environment. Join the club and attend meetings or, better yet, run for a leadership role and you will have an opportunity to speak at every single meeting. Joining Toastmasters was the first thing I did when I started a job that required public speaking skills and I continue to recommend it to clients and friends.

Give a TEDx speech: We'll talk below about how TED has changed the field of speaking. For now, if you have a message you'd like to share with others, find a locally organized TEDx event and contact the curator.[5] The audition process alone will help you hone your skills and your message. My TEDx opportunity came in 2014 and became an amazing reputation-building event. In fact, it was the first time I combined the topics of music and public speaking, kick-starting a new direction for my business and an impactful message for my audience. You can watch that speech at www.speakwithimpactbook.com. ⊕

LEARNING FROM OTHER SPEAKERS

Start to take notice of other speakers. Who do you think is a powerful speaker, and why? Do you resonate with his message? Does she appear genuine and authentic? Does his sense of humor make you laugh and keep you engaged? Take note of the qualities you like in the speaker.

You'll also notice that there are a lot of lackluster speakers out there. As you listen to them, unpack those negative qualities. What bothers you? Does she sound bored and uninterested? Does he appear unsure of himself and his experience? Does she look at the floor instead of at the audience? You can learn a lot from speakers you don't want to emulate. We often pick up the speaking styles of the people around us, for better or for worse. One man I coached spoke with a flat and monotonous voice. When I asked him why, he said,

"Well, that's the way my boss speaks." When he realized that assumption, he was able to unlock the natural range of his voice.

Look at the experts in your industry, your religious and political leaders, or TV personalities, and evaluate why they are effective or ineffective in their speaking. At the end of my workshops, I provide notepads for people to take notes on the speakers they hear. They can also use those notepads to get feedback from colleagues when they give a speech. Download a sample at www.speakwithimpactbook.com. ⊕

The Phenomenon of TED Talks

Begun in 1984 with a focus on Technology, Education, and Design, TED has become an annual conference showcasing innovative speakers and ideas from around the world. [6] In 2006, TED started posting its talks online, which exponentially increased the number of people who could watch and learn from these speakers. In 2009, TEDx became a vehicle for independently organized events under the TED umbrella, spawning a whole new wave of talks and making it easier for both speakers and audience members to attend.

I won't go into what makes a good TED talk, since there are already great books on the subject. One of my favorites, which I've used in my course at the Harvard Kennedy School, is *Talk Like TED* by Carmine Gallo. [7] ⊕

I mention TED for two reasons. First, it provides an endless resource for watching speeches online and learning from speakers. Do you need something to do during a quick break from work? Watch or listen to a TED talk. Second, TED has changed the way people listen to speeches. TED talks have shown us that you can deliver a powerful message in eighteen minutes or less (which makes sense, given that the average adult attention span is up to twenty minutes); [8] this is just as important in a work presentation or community event. TED talks have shown us the power of personal stories to help an audience understand an issue. TED talks have given us permission to speak like real people: in a conversational, personal tone instead of using professional jargon and complex terminology. In fact, the elements of a good TED talk are simply the best practices in public speaking overall.

As a result of TED, audiences have realized that speeches can be both educational and entertaining. We no longer expect boring lectures; we want speeches to keep us engaged even as we are informed. I believe TED talks have changed the expectations of audience members around the world.

CHAPTER 2

Start with Strategy

*The Three Most Important Questions to Ask
Before a Speech or Presentation*

PREPARING TO SPEAK

Let's assume you have a speech or presentation coming up. You're sitting at your desk, scratching your head while looking at a blank screen or sheet of paper, agonizing over what to say. The closer the speech date is, the more pressure you feel. The more important the audience is, the more pressure you feel. All that pressure is enough to make your mind go blank and your heart beat fast. It's almost as if you're experiencing the same fear you'd feel standing onstage.

Let's take a step back.

I'm going to walk you through a series of steps that will guide you painlessly and efficiently through the process of preparing for a speech, presentation, meeting, or phone call. By using this structure, you will find your motivation to speak and kick-start your creativity.

Before you start writing, identify the context of your speech.

- *Where* will you be presenting? Is it a conference or meeting? Where geographically will it take place? Imagine the venue and the setting to put yourself in the minds of your audience members.

- *When* will it take place in the overall agenda? If you are the
  first speaker of the day, your energy will set the tone for the entire day. If you are the last speaker of the day, you have to keep
  up the energy in front of a tired audience who wants to leave
  early to beat the traffic and go home (we'll talk about how to
  engage the audience in Chapter 5).

- *Who else* is speaking? If you're speaking on a controversial subject, will other speakers refute your point of view? Conversely,
  how can you differentiate yourself from other speakers at the
  conference?

At one conference I attended, a magician persuaded the audience
to play a trick on an unsuspecting volunteer by convincing the volunteer that he had vanished onstage (he hadn't). Ironically, the very next
speaker was an expert in trust building, something we very obviously
had *not* done in the previous situation. That's an example of poor
advance planning.

A few more questions about the context of your speech:

- How long will you have to speak? Five minutes, thirty minutes,
  or an hour or more? The duration will help shape your goal.

- Will your speech include time for questions and answers? If so,
  Chapter 10 will help you prepare.

- What does the organizer expect from your speech? Sometimes
  the organizer's expectations differ from yours. Make sure that
  your expectations are in alignment. I will normally ask a
  meeting planner, "What do you want the audience to *do, think,*
  or *feel* as a result of my speech?"

While the above questions are intended for a conference, they
apply to a meeting as well.

The answers also help you prepare to be flexible. Having sat
through numerous meetings, I know that those speaking toward the

end will have their speaking time squeezed as the meeting runs late. One of my clients mentioned that she knows this will happen, so she comes prepared with a "back-pocket edition," a shortened version of her presentation. This lets her calmly and smoothly deliver the most critical information instead of rushing through the entire presentation like an actor accepting an Oscar, racing to include all her *thank-yous* in her Academy Award speech as the music starts to get louder and louder.

Now that you have the context firmly in your mind, it's time to kick-start the creative process.

There are three questions I ask myself before I write any speech or presentation or prepare for a difficult conversation, a client pitch, or speaking up in a meeting. They are so critical, I call them "the Three Questions." They are:

1. Who is your audience?

2. What is your goal?

3. Why you?

The Three Questions are not the structure of your speech; they form the *strategy* of your speech. They warm up your mind and unlock your creativity so you can choose a subject easily and organically. These are the questions that overcome writer's block.

1. WHO IS YOUR AUDIENCE?

"If you talk to a man in a language he understands, that goes to his head. If you talk to him in his own language, that goes to his heart."
—Nelson Mandela[1]

Before you can decide what to say, you need to know whom you are addressing. Your audience can be one person in a corner office, fifteen people in a boardroom, or five hundred people in a ballroom. Are they peers, direct reports, or your company's leadership team? What is their professional background: Are they parents, business executives, or lawyers? Are they all of the same nationality, or are they a diverse group? Do they have the same specialized education as you? Oftentimes, you will have numerous types of people in the audience, but you have one *target* audience.

Now ask yourself who else might see this speech if it's posted online.

We can no longer assume that what we say in a room will stay in that room. An offhand comment in a closed-door meeting can be made public and have disastrous effects. Look at 2012 American presidential candidate Mitt Romney's statement disparaging 47 percent of Americans to see how one comment can elicit major debate.[2] ⊕ Words matter, and they can easily be taken out of context or become the unintended message of your entire campaign.

What Language Do They Speak?

Once you identify your audience, you will know which language to speak. I don't mean which foreign language, although that may certainly be a factor. I mean: Do they speak the specialized language of your industry, of your culture? Will they understand your jargon or acronyms?

Think of how many terms exist in your industry or even within your company. If you use the word "development," will your audience know if it's about real estate, international aid, fund-raising, or software? If you use the acronym SME, will your audience know if you are referring to Small and Medium-Sized Enterprises or Subject-Matter Experts? If people in your audience are unclear as to the meaning, they probably won't raise their hand to ask. Who wants to risk looking foolish in front of their colleagues asking a question they "should" know the answer to? They'll be so distracted by their own feelings of inadequacy that they will have disengaged from the speech.

This doesn't mean you need to get rid of acronyms altogether; simply explain what they mean the first time you use each one.

Will Your Quotations Resonate with Them?

When we speak in a house of worship, it's customary to quote religious scripture. When we give a political speech, we often quote political leaders. The audience and context of the speech dictate our use of language. Quoting a source the audience admires is a great way to build rapport.

At the Harvard Kennedy School in Cambridge, Massachusetts, we use the term "across the river" to refer to the Harvard Business School, which sits across the Charles River in Allston. We often use that phrase to describe the difference between business and government: "Well, here at the Kennedy School we look at economic conditions from a policy perspective, but 'across the river' they do things differently." These phrases have a clear meaning to those "in the know" and can promote a sense of unity and camaraderie with the audience. But outside that circle, those phrases can feel exclusive or confusing.

I once coached a woman who worked for UNICEF, the United Nations International Children's Emergency Fund. She was preparing a major speech to potential donors and talking about UNICEF's life-changing work on the ground in conflict zones. At one point, she said, "We are repatriating children associated with armed groups back to their communities."

I stopped her. "What does that mean?" I asked. She replied, "Well, basically we are sending child soldiers home to their families." That second phrase was so much more powerful.

While the original sentence would have worked well for an internal UNICEF audience, this woman was speaking to individual donors who give out of a sense of personal connection to the mission. You don't pull at someone's heartstrings using jargon; you need to paint a vivid, emotional picture so that the audience can actually *see* the impact of your work. If they can see it, they are more likely to give money toward it.

What Does Your Audience Know About Your Subject?

One of my banking clients said to me: "Next week, I'm presenting to the CEO and CFO of a mid-sized company. The CEO thinks in big-picture terms, while the CFO wants the financial details. Basically, I have to speak two different languages at the same time." We discussed ways she could explain the details and then step back to explain the implications. Another client at that same bank suggested: "Don't just explain the numbers, explain what the numbers *mean*."

When a graduate student and entrepreneur at MIT pitches her high-tech startup idea to investors, how does she describe complex, groundbreaking technology in clear, concise language? When a scientist at the US Food and Drug Administration describes new research affecting the health and safety of the American public, how can he use language that is clear and urgent for policymakers who don't have the same scientific background? When the public affairs staffer at a country's central bank wants to teach better spending habits to the general population, how can she explain micro- and macroeconomic factors in layman's terms? Simply describing the speech in our own language is easy; describing it in a way that our audience will understand takes time and effort.

But the payoff is huge; our success depends on others taking action as a result of our speech. If you want the audience to take action, then you need to speak to them in *their* language. Certainly, we may be called on to speak at an academic conference where everyone speaks the same technical language, but we all appreciate hearing something described in clear, concise terms. I'm not talking about dumbing down your research; I'm talking about clearing away the excess descriptions that are clouding up your speech to arrive at the essence of what you want to say, so you can build a compelling case for it.

How Does Your Audience Feel About You and About Your Subject?

When you walk onstage or into a conference room, people are evaluating your credibility and authority as a speaker. Are you speaking to an audience that is already familiar with your background, or are you addressing a new audience with no idea of who you are? Are you speaking to friends, foes, or undecideds? This information will determine what you say, and how.

One female client I worked with was about to turn fifty. The good news and bad news was: she barely looked thirty. I don't have to tell you why this was good news. Why was it bad news? Because the moment she walked into a room, people assumed she was a junior staffer. She came up with phrases she could put in her introduction that mentioned her "twenty-plus years of experience in this industry" and served as a signal to her audience that she had the credibility to speak to them.

When I wrote and delivered speeches for the Consulate General of Israel in Boston, it was essential to understand how my audience felt about the Middle East conflict. Were they pro-Israel or anti-Israel? Would I be walking into a room full of people who were going to welcome me or reject me before I even said a word? Understanding this would help me prepare for the kinds of questions they would ask and to frame my message in a more inclusive way. If I knew the audience could be hostile to my message, then I could phrase my arguments in a way that took their concerns into account; I could potentially neutralize some of their questions before we got to the Q&A, thereby making the Q&A session more productive. Chapter 10 will give us more tools for handling questions.

How Do You Research Your Audience?

There are numerous ways you can research your audience in advance of the speech. Talk to the event organizer to get a sense of why they invited you to speak. Talk to people who represent the audience. Before all our speeches and training programs, my team and I interview potential audience members to understand the organization's culture, its expectations, and how it has reacted in the past to speakers. Spend time on their website and search for recent news about the organization and its industry.

If you've been invited to speak to a group at one of their regular meetings, attend a meeting in advance. That's what I *should* have done with one particular speech. I was invited to speak at a monthly leadership meeting in the DC area. The organizer briefed me on his expectations: tell them your story, and focus on one particular topic. We agreed that I would talk for about twenty minutes and then make it interactive, even though I *normally* use interaction immediately in my speeches and workshops. During the speech, I could tell that I was losing people. They seemed distant, and I could feel them judging me while I spoke. In a survey afterward, people said, "You should make your speeches more interactive; that's what we expect in these monthly meetings." I was so frustrated. Had I attended even one of these meetings beforehand, I would have known the flow and format.

When you understand your audience, what language they speak, and how they feel about your subject, you can start to craft a message that will resonate with them and inspire them to take action. You will *speak their language*. And if they can understand you, then they are much more likely to listen to you.

In anticipation of your upcoming speech or presentation, take time to analyze the audience and find out as much information as you can about their interests, needs, and goals.

2. WHAT IS YOUR GOAL?

In her book *On Speaking Well*, Peggy Noonan says that every speech has a job to do. "Figure out what the job of your speech is and go do it."[3]

Have you ever sat through a boring presentation with no end in sight, wondering where it was going and how it was relevant to you? *How many times* have you sat through such a presentation? Through this book, we'll make sure you're not one of those speakers.

Every speech is an opportunity to touch people, to educate them, to inspire them, and to influence their behavior for the better. Before you start to write the speech, determine what you want its outcome to be. What do you want people to *do* after hearing you speak? Determine your intended outcome and build toward it in the speech.

Do you want constituents to vote for you?

Do you want venture capitalists to invest in your business?

Do you want prospective clients to buy from you?

Do you want funders to donate to your nonprofit and open doors to their wealthy friends?

Do you want people around the world to know what is going on in your country?

You might decide to *start* the speech with the goal in mind: "I'm standing before you today because I hope to earn your vote in November." Or you might *end* your speech with a clear call to action: "And so, I ask for your vote at the polls in November. Tell your friends and family how important this election is to their future and the future of our country."

I've judged a number of startup competitions and heard hundreds of business pitches. Excited entrepreneurs will stand up and make a persuasive case for a compelling business model based on groundbreaking new technology. But sometimes they will leave off the most important part: the "ask." They fail to say exactly what they need and what they will do with it. The more precise you are with your ask, the easier you make it for people to give you what you want.

In addition to strengthening your opening and closing sentences, having a clear goal helps you determine the content you use in your speech.

If your goal is to build trust with the audience, then what information will demonstrate your ethics? You could include a personal story about a time you learned the value of integrity.

If your goal is to raise money from investors, then what information can you provide that highlights your early success and the promise of your product or service? Find those stories, anecdotes, or outcomes.

If your goal is to open people's eyes to a business threat that no one has considered, what evidence should you provide that shows them that the signs are all around them? Look for statistics, trends, or predictions.

What Are the Audience's Barriers to Action?

Professor Marshall Ganz of the Harvard Kennedy School teaches about the importance of understanding people's barriers to action, especially when fostering social change. When you determine the goal of your speech, try to determine your audience's barriers to action. What's holding them back? Could it be politically risky to adopt this new policy? Are you asking people to do something that will make them look foolish in front of their friends and colleagues? Do people lack the money to give? Are you asking people to do something they simply don't have the time to do? Understanding what is holding your audience back helps you come up with a realistic and actionable goal.

For instance, if you are speaking at a political rally, think of some easy steps your audience members can take. Instead of asking them to become full-time volunteers for your campaign, ask them to follow you on social media and share your content with their followers. Ask them to bring a friend to the next rally or make a small donation. The easier you make it for people to take action, the more likely they are to take that action.

How Do You Want People to Feel?

In thinking about the goal of your speech, ask yourself how you want people to feel at the end. Do you want them to feel inspired and up-lifted? Challenged and determined? Knowledgeable and ready?

Nearly all my team's workshops end with a survey requesting feed-back from the audience. The most important question on that survey is: "How do you feel after this workshop?" The answers to that question help us gauge the success of that workshop. If people respond with: tired, overwhelmed, or hungry, then we have some work to do to make the workshop more engaging. Luckily, people usually respond with: confi-dent, inspired, or empowered. Those responses remind me of the power of these workshops and reinforce my commitment to help others.

Where Can You "Give the Work Back"?

As speakers, we are tempted to walk into a room ready to present all the answers to a particular challenge. We sit in our office, think about the challenge, and develop a solution that we then present to our col-leagues to take action. You feel this pressure especially when you're presenting to people you lead. However, when the solution requires other people taking action, then the more you include those people in the solution, the more committed they will be.

I once worked with an executive who needed to address a core group of individuals within his organization. The head of the organi-zation had just chastised this group, and now this executive was deal-ing with the aftermath. As we prepared the content of the speech, we realized that he couldn't just walk in there and present a solution. The managers themselves probably had valuable ideas on how to find a solution. So instead of planning a formal speech to this group, we drafted a *conversation starter* that demonstrated his faith in those managers and his belief that they had all the tools they needed to find a solution. He then opened the meeting up for them to discuss ideas and together talk about how to move forward.

In their book *Leadership on the Line*, my professor Ronald Heifetz from the Harvard Kennedy School and his co-author, Marty Linsky, call this "giving the work back."[4] Instead of the stoic leader trying to come up with the perfect solution to a challenge facing an organization or community, they talk about including the community itself in finding the solution. You give the work—finding a solution—back to the people who are most likely to have the best answers. This strategy helps you solicit ideas from people on the ground, receive critical feedback, empower others to speak up, and gain valuable buy-in. As we discussed earlier, giving a speech is not just to impart information; it's to empower people to work together to solve a challenge. Before you speak, look at ways to bring others into your leadership strategy to make your message more impactful.

In anticipation of your upcoming speech, think about the goal of the speech. What do you want people to do and feel? How can you bring them into the solution? Write that down.

3. WHY YOU?

What gets you out of bed in the morning? What made you choose your line of work? What made you volunteer for this particular cause? Why do you do what you do? In other words, *Why you?*

Why you? is the single most powerful question you can ask yourself when preparing a speech or presentation. This is where you put aside the bureaucracy of your job, the politics of your cause, or the dysfunction of your office, and determine the sense of purpose that guides your actions.

It's not "So I can make more money" or "So I can get promoted" or "So I can look good in front of my boss." It's deeper than that. And you might have to ask yourself this question repeatedly to get the underlying answer.

In one of our leadership communication training programs, my team and I coach the sales managers of a financial institution. I was helping one particular mid-level manager prepare for an upcoming sales call. I asked her, "Why you? Why do you do what you do?"

She responded, "Well, I like serving others."

"*Why?*"

"Because I believe in service."

"Why?"

"Because service is important to me."

"Why?"

"Because that's what my parents taught me."

"Tell me more."

"Growing up, my parents ran their own business. Every single day, I saw them get up early to serve their customers, putting others' needs before their own. I think about that experience every day when I wake up, and I want to teach that to my children as well. That's why I do what I do." *A-hah!*

Do you see how we had to dig down a few layers there? We had to get past the generic answer to arrive at the underlying drivers of her behavior.

In another training program, one woman got straight to the point when she said, "My father sold insurance, and every day he came home happy. When it was time to choose a career, I chose to follow in his footsteps. That's why I do what I do."

You'll notice a lot of the *Why you?* comes back to family and early childhood. You might think it's unprofessional to share a personal story in a business setting. But we are not robots; we are human beings doing business with other human beings. We are driven by personal motivations, and we have values that guide our actions. When you share those motivations with others, even in a business setting, you connect on a personal level and you build trust.

One of the best places to include your *Why you?* is in the beginning of your speech or presentation. Imagine using the story about growing up in a family-owned business when you are pitching a small business prospect. Using that story, the prospect might think, "Yes, this person understands where I am coming from. I can trust this person."

There are many different advantages to having a *Why you?*

It helps you choose language that is authentic to you. It's hard to sound authentic when you are parroting corporate jargon. *Why you?* brings out your natural language and makes your speech more genuine.

It animates your body and voice. In Chapter 6, we will learn how body language and vocal tone can complement your message. When you truly believe in your message, that sense of purpose animates your body and voice naturally.

It builds your confidence. Both young professionals and seasoned executives will confess to a lack of confidence when speaking. What if others in the room know more than I do? What if the audience is questioning my authority to speak? Connecting with your *Why you?* reinforces your credibility and your authority.

I remember a young woman from Egypt in one of my workshops at Harvard. She had written a very general speech about the dangers of revolutions. She was too nervous to speak, and finally asked me in front of the class: "Why would anybody want to listen to me? I'm only nineteen years old."

I responded to her: "You have lived through a revolution. You have more personal credibility than someone with a PhD in the subject." She thought about that for a moment, then stood up and gave one of the most passionate, personal speeches I have ever heard, telling her own story. She had to give herself permission to speak.

Why you? is the most powerful question you can ask when preparing a speech, presentation, or conversation. It centers you, calms you, and helps you connect with a sense of purpose.

Sometimes *Why you?* can be hard to find.

I remember coaching a man who worked in real estate development. I knew this was an engaged, passionate individual with a fabulous sense of humor. But as he stood up to practice a presentation to a community board, he changed completely. His shoulders slumped, his smile drooped into a grimace, and he sighed loudly while leaning on one hip and weakly gesturing at the slides behind him. He was afraid that he was a boring speaker. And actually, *he was.* So we worked through the Three Questions, and when we arrived at *Why you?* he came to a startling realization. I asked him why he was passionate about his work. It turns out, *he wasn't.* He hated his job. He mistrusted his boss. He didn't like the industry. He wasn't a boring speaker, he was just *bored.*

If you are bored with your subject or if you hate your job, it's going to be very difficult to give a powerful, authentic speech. And in those cases, you do have a couple of options. You can change careers, as my friend did. He wound up quitting his job and pursuing his dream to revitalize an abandoned building in his city. But maybe you have three kids to support, college bills, and a mortgage. So instead of searching for what you're passionate about, think about what you *like* about your work.

Working with investment bankers, I sometimes find resistance to the word "passion." They'll say, "I work hundred-hour weeks in a high-stress environment. I'm not just doing it for the money, but I wouldn't exactly say I'm passionate about it. I *do* like being able to solve problems for my clients. It's like a puzzle, and I like putting together the pieces of the puzzle." That works.

You can find your *"Why you?"* in a few different ways. Ask yourself:

- Why do you care about your audience or about the occasion of the speech?

- Why do you care about your subject or your organization?

- What are you proud of in your work?

How will you know when you find the answer that resonates? You'll know, because you'll feel it and think, "Yes, that's the thing I'm looking for."

Now that you've researched your audience and determined the goal of your speech, ask yourself *"Why you?"* Speak it out loud before you write it down. Ask it a few times to go deeper into your motivation, and then try to explain it further. Share it with a trusted friend or colleague. You'll know when you've found it.

DETERMINING YOUR MAIN MESSAGE

Once you've asked yourself the Three Questions, you're ready to determine the main message of your speech. In fact, now it should be much easier to arrive at the message.

Imagine an audience member leaving your speech. She goes into an elevator, and someone asks her, "What was that speech about?" Her answer should be your main message. The main message should be relevant and compelling to your audience; what will they get out of the speech? Be explicit.

"In today's presentation, I'll show you how to improve client satisfaction in a way that helps you retain more clients, get more referrals, and exceed your sales goals."

"Every single one of us will feel the effects of climate change, and we have to act before it's too late."

"If we work on our company culture, then business growth will follow."

When you focus on a single message, you increase the power of that message. When you throw in five different messages, you dilute each one.

Write your main message in one sentence and read it out loud. It can be a compound sentence, but keep it short and simple. What are you going to talk about, and why is it important to your audience?

CHAPTER 3

Write the Speech

A Process to Write Any Speech or Presentation

FINDING THE RIGHT TIME

Are you an early riser who gets more done between 8 a.m. and 11 a.m. than most people in an entire day? Or do you only truly wake up in the afternoon, and 10 p.m. is your productive time? Whichever time you prefer, *that's* when you should write your speech or presentation.

I come from a long line of early birds, and I'm no exception. My mother says that, by 10 a.m., the day is half over. If I sit down to write a speech at 4 p.m , it's going to feel like an uphill battle. My mind will be overwhelmed by everything that's already happened that day, my energy level will be sinking into the ground, and I'll be hungry and distracted. That's not the best state of mind to do my most creative work.

As you prepare to write, look at your calendar and block off time during your most productive time of day. In fact, while you're in your calendar, look at the date of your upcoming speech, and block off time to practice it.

How far in advance of your speech should you start to prepare? The amount of time you spend depends on two major factors: how important the speech occasion is, and how often you have spoken on the subject.

Imagine you've just been promoted to the head of a line of business within your multinational corporation. You're speaking at a company off-site to about two hundred leaders, and the CEO of the corporation is there. Your job is to inspire your new leadership team and talk about your vision for the coming year. Time to start preparing: one month in advance.

Now imagine you're presenting the findings of a project you've been working on for the past few weeks. You're speaking to a group of colleagues who know you, like you, and just need a quick update. You know exactly what you want to say—in fact, you gave this exact presentation last week to another group. Time to start preparing: one day before.

Writing a speech or presentation is an iterative process, so I recommend working on it in blocks of time. Spend forty-five minutes, take a break, and then come back. Give yourself time to think about the material, and then come back the next day with a fresh head. Unfortunately, most people have no process at all. They stress about the presentation for weeks without actually doing anything; and when they do sit down to write, their mind goes blank. Finally, the night before the event, in a fit of desperation, they come up with something they can say and spend all night adjusting text boxes in their slide deck because it's too late to ask someone else to do it, only to come in the next morning exhausted and think, "Let's just get it over with already."

Or, worse, they don't prepare at all and just try to wing it. That's when they stand in front of their peers and start *umm*-ing and *ahh*-ing as they wait for a flash of inspiration to strike.

In this book, I give you a repeatable process you can use to prepare for every speech, presentation, or conversation, no matter how much time you have.

Do you like to write on a sheet of paper, or a digital device?

There's no wrong answer: whatever works for you is what you should use. If you use a device, simply make sure you're saving your work constantly and backing it up.

Can you write from your office? If you're in a cubicle or shared workspace, that might be difficult. Maybe you're the kind of person who finds inspiration in the white noise of a coffee shop or who can sit out on your back porch. Or maybe you need the complete silence of a library. There's no wrong answer; there's only what works for you.

As you prepare for the writing process, make sure you are in the right mental space. If you meditate, spend some time in meditation beforehand. Make sure you're fed, caffeinated if necessary, and comfortable so you don't get distracted. And turn off all your digital distractions: turn off message notifications, put your phone on silent with no vibration, and close your door.

Should you write together with someone else? It can be helpful to brainstorm your speech topic and your message with a friend or colleague who knows the audience. My coaches and I spend a lot of time helping our clients answer the Three Questions and craft their main message. If you're giving a group presentation, answer the Three Questions together with your group, and then decide who is taking what section of the presentation.

Should you work with a speechwriter? I've served as a speechwriter in the past, and now I recommend people work with professional speechwriters when they have an important speech and don't have the time or bandwidth to write it themselves, or if they are in an executive role where they are constantly speaking in high-stakes situations.

Stephen Krupin, a White House speechwriter to President Barack Obama and currently the head of the executive communications practice at SKDKnickerbocker, says, "Your story is only as good as your ability to tell it to the stakeholders who matter. When speechwriters look at a collection of ideas, data, and anecdotes, we can see an argument that will grab someone's attention and move them to act."

Matthew Rees, a White House speechwriter to President George W. Bush and currently the founder of the speechwriting firm GEO-NOMICA, offers this guidance when working with a speechwriter: "Communicate to the writer the content you'd like to have included (you'd be surprised how rarely this happens). A meeting or phone call can suffice, but most effective is preparing an outline for the speech, as this ensures nothing gets lost in translation. Share your previous speeches or articles, as well as articles that you think are relevant to the topic you'll be covering. Speechwriters have many talents, but they're not mind readers. The more guidance you give them, the more likely it will be that they give you a speech that you actually want to deliver."

Determine the best time of day to write your speech. Look at the speech date on your calendar and block off times to prepare. Think of the best place to write, and ask yourself if you should engage the help of a speechwriter. Talk through ideas with a friend, colleague, or coach.

BRAINSTORMING THE CONTENT

Everyone has their own writing process. I'm going to share with you my process and the one my team and I use with our clients. You are free to use it or adapt it to your own needs. Whether you write the script word-for-word or just use bullet points depends on how comfortable you are with the material. Regardless of what you choose when you write, reduce your speech to bullet points before the day of the speech.

Start by reviewing the Three Questions: *Who is your audience? What is your goal? Why you?* Then read through your one-sentence main message. Adjust it if necessary.

What comes next is critical and should not be interrupted. *Just write.*

Brainstorm everything you would want to say on the topic, all the main points, and all your ideas about the subject. *Just write.*

Think of all the relevant stories or examples you could share on the topic. *Just write.*

Think of what was in the news about your subject lately and any interesting facts. *Just write.*

Don't judge, don't edit, and don't think about what others will think of you. *Just write.*

In his book *On Writing*, Stephen King says, "Write with the door closed, rewrite with the door open."[1] Write for yourself, then edit for others. This process is so important because it's usually our judgment and self-awareness that holds us back from writing.

Once you've finished writing, read it to make sure you got everything out of your head and onto paper or screen.

Then take a break. Physically get up and walk around. Get a drink, use the restroom, and go outside for a breath of fresh air.

Congratulations! You've finished the hardest part of the writing process.

During your most productive time of day, ask the Three Questions and then brainstorm your speech without interruptions or judgment. *Just write.*

FINDING THE RIGHT STRUCTURE

Look at the content with a critical eye. Now you can "rewrite with the door open," as Stephen King says. Look through your text and pick out the key arguments. Which are the most compelling points for your audience? How do you rearrange them into a structure?

One of my favorite structures is called Monroe's Motivated Sequence: a five-step outline developed by Purdue University professor Alan Monroe in the 1930s. I learned it from the book *The Political Speechwriter's Companion* by Robert Lehrman.[2] The book, which I highly recommend even for those outside politics, delves in more depth into this structure.

Monroe's Motivated Sequence

1. *Attention:* Grab the audience's attention immediately.

2. *Need or Problem:* What is the problem you are addressing?

3. *Satisfaction or Solution:* What is the solution you are proposing?

4. *Visualization:* What will the world look like if you are successful? Or unsuccessful? Paint a picture.

5. *Action:* What is your call to action for the audience?

Let's choose a message and use Monroe's Motivated Sequence to outline the structure.

Message: Together, we can eradicate homelessness in the United States.

To help craft this message, I call my friend and colleague Jacki Coyle, Executive Director of Shepherd's Table in Silver Spring, Maryland. Shepherd's Table is a local community organization that supports men and women experiencing homelessness by providing basic human services such as meals, clothing, and crisis intervention, among many other services.

1. *Attention:* Last night, the temperature fell below freezing. How many of you would sleep outside in this weather? I didn't think so. Imagine if you had to sleep outside with only a flattened cardboard box separating you from the frozen pavement. How well would you sleep? Think of the emotional cost of being on the street: the fear and lack of self-esteem. Now imagine you had a job interview this morning so you could earn enough money to rent an apartment and get off the streets. How confident would you feel that you could ace that interview and land the job? [*shaking head*] I didn't think so.

2. *Problem:* At any given point in time, there could be half a million people experiencing homelessness in the United States.[3] This includes people who are sleeping on the street, in transitional housing, or in emergency shelters. Without permanent and affordable housing, they are held hostage to an endless cycle from which they can't break free. Affordable housing is crucial for them to get back on their feet. This is not something that happens far away from our communities; it happens literally right on our doorsteps.

3. *Solution:* We can't just wait for others to fix the problem; we are all stakeholders. We all have a part to play, whether we work in federal, state, and local governments, whether we are landlords, developers, donors, or simply concerned citizens. The solution to homelessness will happen when everyone combines their skills and their resources to confront the problem. Helping those who are most vulnerable improves life not only for them but also for the community at large. It affects all of us.

4. *Visualization:* Now imagine that instead of sleeping on the cold pavement last night, you slept in a warm bed. Your name is on the lease. Your self-esteem has improved, and your emotional and physical energy is replenished. You feel like part of your community. You are ready to ace that interview.

5. *Action:* Each one of us can make this vision a reality. If you're a landlord, set aside housing for people in need, knowing that there are government programs to reimburse you. If you are in local government, protect and expand those programs. And if you're an individual, get involved: volunteer, learn the issues, meet the people, and use your voice to change the systems that keep people on the street. Together, we can eradicate homelessness in the United States.

Pretty powerful, right? You could use that structure with *any message*, whether you're running for office, advocating for a new business strategy, or persuading your community to save a historic building.

If I'm not using Monroe's Motivated Sequence, I might simply use the rule of three: introduction, three main points, and conclusion. Or I might use a chronological structure: past, present, and future. Once I brainstorm what I want to say, the structure usually emerges from the content, and that structure guides the audience through the speech.

Focus on Signposts

Simply having the right structure does not ensure a compelling speech. We also need to spend time on the transitions between points: building momentum from one point to the next, and taking the audience on a journey. I'm a big fan of using rhetorical questions as transitions. You can ask questions like, "How does this apply to us?" to transition from theory to practice, or, "What's our next step?" to transition to action items. These transitions are called "signposts." Other signposts include structural phrases such as: "I'm going to talk about three things today: first . . . second . . . and finally . . ." Putting your structure into words at the beginning of your speech provides clarity for your audience and keeps them engaged throughout.

When we read a written report, we know where it starts and ends. We know where Chapter 1 ends and Chapter 2 begins, and we can look ahead to see how long it's going to take to read it. In a speech or presentation, the signposts tell your audience where they are and where they are going. It's as if you're taking the audience on a journey through the woods. If you simply walk them down a long dirt road, with no mile markers or indications of their progress, they start to get distracted. They feel tired and hungry. But if there are signposts such as a map up front and mile markers along the way, they can see their progress and understand how close they are to the end. Don't leave them wandering in the woods.

Research Your Subject

At this point in your speech, you might find areas that need more research. Maybe you're talking about a groundbreaking new medicine and want to see what has been done to date. Maybe you quote a colleague and want to make sure that quote is accurate (and that you have her permission to say it). Now is the time to fact-check the material and make sure you're saying exactly what you want to say. Think about the speech being posted online—what do you need to adjust so that your speech can stand the test of time?

There are endless ways for you to research your subject. You can easily get lost in articles, papers, and studies, and lose precious time that you could have spent preparing. In fact, when people *over*-prepare, they usually over-research their subject.

When researching a speech subject, I like to interview experts. Not only do I find quotes for the speech, but I also build my professional network. You could read books on your subject, though you may not have the time before a speech. If you have a research assistant, you can ask him or her to read the book and summarize the key points for you. If you have access to academic journals, you can look at past studies on your subject. And, of course, you can search online for your subject, though be sure to check the validity of the source before you use it. Check news sources about your subject to see what the latest developments or controversies are. These research methods will also help you anticipate questions or audience pushback.

Read the Speech Out Loud

I can always tell when someone has written a speech but never read it out loud, because it will contain words that are written for the eye and not the ear. Journalists know how to write a beautiful, eloquent sentence that provides history, context, and nuance. Read a newspaper article out loud and you'll see what I mean. Writing for the eye and the ear are two very different methods and require different phrasing, pacing, and language. When you write a business report, you tend to use your organization's jargon. Yet a speech is an opportunity to build a relationship with your audience, so your spoken language should be more authentic.

Once you finish the first draft of your speech, read it out loud and ask yourself how it sounds. Does it sound natural? Do the words feel comfortable? Is there a more concise phrase you can use?

If you're giving a speech in a foreign language, pay extra attention to the words you use. Because that language doesn't come naturally to you, it's important to find words that feel comfortable to pronounce. If you stumble over a word while practicing, you're likely to stumble over that word in the speech itself. Chapter 11 provides more strategies for speaking in a foreign language.

I was once coaching an international student at Harvard University who was giving the Graduate Student Oration at commencement. This is a huge honor and also a very high-stakes experience, speaking in front of thirty thousand students and parents in Harvard Yard while the event is streamed live on Harvard's website. Intimidating? Just a bit.

This young man, a scientist, had a heavy foreign accent and, during our coaching, was getting tripped up on the word "manipulate." We practiced it a few times, and he always stumbled. Finally, I asked him, "Is there another word you could use instead?" He furrowed his brow as he thought about it for a minute; then his face brightened and he said, "Control!" We changed the word in his speech, and he breezed through the sentence.

Trust yourself. Read your speech out loud and if something doesn't feel right, change it. The less you concentrate on those individual words, the more you can focus on your message.

> Once you brainstorm your speech, go through it to determine the best structure. Plan your transitions from one point to the next, and do extra research if you need to shore up your knowledge. Read it out loud to make sure it sounds like your natural language.

ADDING AN OPENING AND CLOSING

Now that you've written the body of your speech, it's time to think strategically about your opening and closing phrases. They could each comprise one sentence or one paragraph; it depends on the tools you use.

Think about the last time you heard a speech or presentation. What were you doing while the speaker was walking onstage or preparing to present? You might have been checking your phone to make sure your spouse dropped off the kids at school or to see if your prospect had responded to that big proposal you sent.

The opening of a speech grabs the audience's attention and tells them to *stop what they are doing and listen*. The opening piques people's curiosity, convinces them of your authority to speak, and starts to build a relationship with the audience.

The First Eight Seconds

I once interviewed a venture capitalist named David Wells, who was a partner at Kleiner Perkins Caufield & Byers, as I prepared to coach a group of entrepreneurs on their pitches. I asked David what he was looking for when listening to a pitch, since he listens to hundreds of pitches and makes decisions that affect millions of dollars. He said something I will never forget.

David said, "Within the first eight words, I've decided whether or not to keep listening."

I paused, unsure I had heard right.

"Eight words?" I repeated uneasily.

"Eight words," he responded firmly.

"What are you looking for in those eight words?" I finally asked.

He replied, "The core innovation. If it's not in the first eight words, it's probably not there. That's when I either stop listening or interrupt the speaker to ask."

Does it sound unfair that someone would give you so little time before making a decision about your future? I agree with you; but let's step back to look at David's larger point. The first sentence of your presentation is critical, especially if you're speaking to an audience that doesn't know you and that is listening to dozens of other people just like you.

A couple of years after that meeting with David, I was on a flight from Washington, DC, to Sarasota, Florida, and sat next to a professional comedian. Tim the Dairy Farmer speaks at agricultural conferences around the country. Fascinated by both his line of work and his specialization, I peppered him with questions about his technique, his strategy, and his experience. He said something that made me recall David's point years before.

Tim said that, when he walks onstage, he has to bond with the audience within the first eight seconds of his act. He sets the mood for the entire show in those first eight seconds. "If you walk onstage looking nervous, then the audience will feel nervous. If you smile, on the other hand, it invites your audience in." In fact, his goal is to make the audience laugh every eight seconds throughout the entire show.

While the average adult attention span is up to twenty minutes, continuous attention spans can last as short a time as eight seconds.[4] Those eight words were starting to look less extreme and more logical.

Let's imagine that you're a government contractor pitching to a federal agency. There are a half dozen other contractors bidding for the same project, presenting one after the other. Should you pay close attention to your first eight seconds so you can demonstrate how you are different? Let's ask the client.

A friend of mine works for a US government agency and has been listening to pitches for over fifteen years. He says, "We know that capabilities are often similar across service providers. What we're looking for are indicators that we're going to work well with this team: the intro, the follow-up, and their ability to connect with their customer. The relationship is important to us." For him, the first eight seconds happens before the contractors even start talking. He looks at how they interact with his administrative assistant before they start. She'll come in with an expression on her face based on how she was treated in the lobby.

Don't let this focus on eight seconds overwhelm you when you think about your opening. Instead, let it remind you of the importance of being purposeful in your opening. More than "So . . . yeah."

Ways to Open Your Speech

Your opening depends on the audience and the goal of the speech.

Greeting. Many people ask me: *Is it okay to open your speech with "good morning" or "good afternoon"?* Yes, there's nothing wrong with a warm, confident greeting that tells your audience you are ready to begin. When I'm speaking to an audience in a foreign country, I like to greet them in their language as a sign of respect, making sure to pronounce the words correctly.

Personally, I don't like it when speakers say "Good morning! I can't hear you. GOOD MORNING!" It makes me feel like they are chastising the audience, and it puts me on the defensive. I also don't recommend starting with thank-yous. It doesn't grab people's attention, and it doesn't support the main message of your speech. Leave the thank-yous for the end.

Quotation. There's an incredible energy that comes from walking onstage, pausing, looking directly at your audience, and using a powerful quote. Remember your audience and your goal when choosing a quote. If you're speaking at an internal conference, you can quote someone well known within the company. If you're speaking to a religious community, you can quote religious scripture. You can also use a surprising quote to startle your audience. I remember visiting a Toastmasters meeting where the speaker started with a series of illogical misstatements from an unnamed US presidential candidate on the campaign trail. The mostly Democratic audience smirked, assuming the misstatements had come from Republican president George W. Bush. Then the speaker revealed that those statements came from Democratic presidential candidate Barack Obama. The audience's surprise made them pay attention to what the speaker said next.

Visualization. I'd like you to close your eyes for a minute and imagine that you are walking into the local branch of your bank. You know your banker by name and usually wait only a couple of minutes before you can speak to her. But this time is different. You walk into the bank, and there's a long line of people impatiently waiting for their turn. You wait for twenty minutes and start to feel like you're no longer a valued customer. One of my banking clients came up with that visualization when preparing to speak to colleagues about the importance of client satisfaction. It served as a powerful reminder to focus on the client experience instead of simply cutting costs. Visualizations help you transport the audience to a different place and time, enabling them to see what you see and feel what you feel. Our brains react to those visualizations as if we had experienced them ourselves, as we'll see in Chapter 4 when we talk about storytelling.

Statistics. Used in moderation, statistics can capture your audience's attention and elaborate on the message of your speech. They can be used to create urgency: "Look around the room. One in three of you will be diagnosed with cancer during your lifetime."[5] Or to pull at people's heartstrings: "Over half of the world's refugees are children."[6] A few well-placed statistics can set the stage for your message.

Story. Several years ago, I was struggling to write the intro for a workshop I would give in McAllen, Texas. I was born in the northeastern US, and this was my first trip to Texas. I was trying to think of a way for a Northerner to connect with a southern audience. So I did a little research on McAllen and realized that I had distant relatives there whom I had never met. So I started my speech with the following story:

"My great-grandmother had eight brothers and sisters. In the early 1900s, each one left Poland and settled along the Americas: New York, Mexico, Cuba, Costa Rica, and Argentina. A few weeks ago, I told my father about my visit here, and he revealed that part of our family had *actually moved to McAllen*! I don't know where they are, and I've never met them. So although this is my first trip to McAllen, it feels like coming home." The audience relaxed, and I felt like I was able to connect with them immediately.

And it didn't end there. After the program, a man approached me. He whispered intently: "Are you Jewish? There aren't many of us here in McAllen. What's your family's name?" I provided the name, and his face brightened immediately: "He's my neighbor! Would you like his phone number?" Later that afternoon, I met one of my distant cousins for the first time. He told me the backstory of our family history, filling in details from the past hundred years. I was stunned and appreciative. Using a personal story has the immediate benefit of helping you connect with your audience. It can also lead to surprising connections.

How Not to Open a Speech

Performers live by the saying "The show must go on." If you're sick or didn't get a chance to practice the day before, you can't use that as an excuse. Many people will start with, "I just found out last night that I had to give this speech," or, "Bear with me, I'm not feeling that well today." We use these statements to lower people's expectations, but what we're really saying is, "I'm sorry, you are not going to hear a good speech today." Most of the time, the audience doesn't know when you feel sick or when you're unprepared. Most of the time, they don't know you've made a mistake until you tell them—either with your words (an apology) or your face (a grimace). In our workshops, people have ten minutes to write a speech that they will deliver on the spot. Half of the speeches are so good that no one would have ever known they had been written within the past hour. Pause and breathe before you speak, then get out there and speak. The show must go on.

Ways to Close Your Speech

The end of a speech is a powerful time to underscore your message and leave your audience with a compelling call to action. In my experience, people don't spend enough time preparing that last part of their speech. They expect a stroke of brilliance to come in the moment, but they wind up rambling as their voice trails off, repeating the same thing while the audience wonders when the speech will end.

The end of your speech is an opportunity to make your audience feel, think, or act in a certain way. Depending on what you want them to feel, think, or do, choose the speech closing accordingly.

All the speech openers we discussed above can be used to close a speech.

Do you want them to feel a sense of hope? Use an inspirational quote or a visualization, painting a picture of the world as it could be. Look for quotes that are unique, as opposed to something the audience will have heard many times before.

Do you want them to feel more connected to you personally? Use a story that helps them relate to you and that also reinforces the message of your speech. If you used a story in the beginning, then reference that story again at the end, especially if there's a twist that you can use to support your message. One of my students started her speech with a story about a time when she was a little girl. The speech then focused on her goal of eradicating poverty in her country. She ended the speech by referencing how that little girl would feel today.

Do you want them to do something? Include a call to action that's logical and easy for the audience to take. This is where the goal of your speech is critical. Do you want the audience to vote for you? Make the request at the end of your speech. Do you want them to invest in you? Make a clear ask for funds and say what you'll use them for. Do you want them to understand an issue? Summarize the main points of the issue and talk about the implications for the future.

When you near the end of the speech, speak slowly and clearly. You'll be tempted to let your voice trail off at the end, but resist that urge. What you say will be powerful, and you want people to hear and feel it. Let your voice rise and fall for each sentence, and slow down in the last sentence so it can really sink in.

Should You Say "Thank You"?

Sometimes I like to thank audiences at the end of the speech. It's a clear way of telling people that you are done, although your tone of voice should also reflect the end of the speech. If you didn't thank the organizers in the beginning, right before your conclusion is a good place to do so; the thank yous should precede your conclusion. What you shouldn't do is quietly mumble "thank you" and then run off the stage. If you're going to thank the audience, pause, look at your audience, and say it with purpose.

Once you've written the bulk of your speech, focus on your opening and closing statements. Use the above techniques to capture your audience's attention, reinforce your main message, and provide a call to action. It's hard to sit down and find inspiration for the opening and conclusion; you might need to get up, go for a walk, and see if inspiration hits. Give it time.

HOW TO WRITE A SPEECH IN THIRTY MINUTES

What do you do when you only have thirty minutes to prepare a speech? The Speechwriting Roadmap is a quick-and-easy formula I've developed for my clients. For a fillable PDF version, visit www.speakwithimpactbook.com.

1. *Focus:* Find a quiet place and silence all your digital devices and notifications.

2. *Ask yourself the Three Questions:* Who is your audience? What is your goal? Why you?

3. *Determine your main message:* In one sentence, what is the main message of your speech?

4. *Brainstorm:* Write out your main points. Don't worry about the order, just brainstorm.

5. *Structure:* From those main points, choose three that best reinforce your main message; this is your structure.

6. *Cut:* Cut out all the extra information that doesn't reinforce your main message.

7. *Write your opening and conclusion:* Think about how you will open and close the speech to capture your audience's attention.

8. *Create bullet points:* In bullet points, create a final document with your opening, three main points, and closing. Think about how you will transition from one point to the next.

9. *Read it out loud:* Print out your bullet points, read your speech out loud, and make sure it sounds like *your* words, *your* voice.

10. *Practice, practice, practice:* Practice the speech in front of a mirror, colleague, or video.

You are ready to go!

CHAPTER 4

Empower Your Audience

Critical Tools to Connect with Your Audience

THE POWER OF PERSUASION

Every speech is an opportunity to influence people's behavior: the way they think, the way they feel, or the way they act. Sounds like manipulation, doesn't it? Unfortunately, sometimes it is. For centuries, dictators and bigots have used speech to incite people to violence, turn them against one another, and foster hatred. And they still do, both online and in person. Public speaking is a tool, and it can be used for good or for evil. I present here tools of persuasion that you can use in your speeches, presentations, and conversations, and I ask you to use them responsibly. Recognize the power you have when you speak in front of a group, and use that power for good.

The second of the Three Questions is, *What is your goal?* That goal usually involves some sort of influence. Even an informational presentation should persuade your audience that you are a credible source and that your information is accurate.

Thousands of years after it was written, we continue to reference Aristotle's *Rhetoric* and the three modes of persuasion he describes.[1] He writes that speakers persuade an audience through a combination of three elements: ethos, logos, and pathos.

Ethos

Whenever you speak in front of an audience, your credibility and authority do a lot of the talking. If you are viewed as credible and knowledgeable, then your audience will be more inclined to listen to you. Perhaps it's your title of CEO that led to the speaking invitation you received. But your ethos doesn't just come from your title. It comes from your experience. Maybe you're new to the company but you have twenty years of experience in the field: that experience is part of your ethos.

When you are nervous before a speech, reminding yourself of your ethos is an important confidence-booster: "I've been researching this subject for twenty years. I've got this." A lack of ethos can also lead to a lack of confidence: "I just graduated from college; why should anyone listen to me?" In that case, the third of the Three Questions, *Why you?*, will help build your confidence because it comes from your passion about your subject.

Logos

The words you use matter. Your language and argumentation matter. Logos is about your ability to craft a logical argument and present facts that reinforce your position. When your speech rambles with no end in sight and your arguments don't make sense, you lack logos and are less persuasive. We've all sat through those kinds of presentations.

To many, logos is the most obvious of the three modes of persuasion. In fact, some people think that a logo is the *only* mode of persuasion, but facts alone rarely persuade an audience. In fact, confirmation bias shows us that when we are confronted with facts that contradict our beliefs, we reject them and hold even more firmly to our beliefs.[2] If you've ever tried to win a political argument with an ideologically opposed uncle, you've quickly learned the uselessness of facts, especially when he seems to have his own. Facts and logic are a crucial component of your persuasive argument, but they will be even more powerful when you include the third mode: pathos.

Pathos

If you don't believe in what you are saying, you can't persuade others. If you don't care about your subject, then your audience won't care either. This isn't about the content; it's about your passion for or interest in the content.

Pathos appeals to people's emotions, and emotion is a very strong persuasive element. I mentioned earlier that a speech is an opportunity to build a relationship of trust with your audience: we do that by showing that we are real people with real emotions. Emotions are universal. No matter which country you live in or what language you speak, everyone can relate to feelings of fear, love, hope, or loss. Telling a personal story is one example of using pathos; asking the audience to imagine a vivid scenario is another. After describing statistics to illustrate a trend, a single story can make those statistics come alive with meaning.

Ethos, logos, pathos. How do you decide which to use? A powerful speech or presentation has some combination of all three, and the exact balance depends on your audience and your goal. Who are you speaking to and what do they relate to? If you're speaking to a skeptical audience that doesn't know you, focus on your credibility: ethos. If you're speaking to a group of facts-driven scientists, include a solid argument in favor of your position: logos. If you're speaking to a group of concerned parents, include an emotional appeal to their desire to protect their children: pathos. There is also overlap among these three modes: your facts can provide an emotional wake-up call and your credibility can come from a personal story.

Five Elements of Persuasion

In my fifteen years of experience in helping clients craft persuasive messages, I've found that an argument is persuasive when it answers five questions that your audience is thinking:

1. **Why you?** Why do you as the speaker care about this subject? If *you* don't care about the subject, then you can't persuade your *audience* to care.

2. **Why me?** Why should your audience care about this subject? Make it relevant to them.

3. **Why now?** What makes this argument urgent and timely? Convince your audience to take action now.

4. **Why bother?** Will we even be able to make any change? Give your audience hope for a positive outcome.

5. **Okay, so what's next?** What should we do? Give the audience a specific call to action. The easier you make it for the audience to take action, the more likely they will be to do it.

When you craft a persuasive argument, try to answer those questions as well. You'll find you can easily integrate them into Monroe's Motivated Sequence or any other structure.

In addition to answering those key questions, there are specific tools that you can use to make a speech or presentation more persuasive.

Tools of Persuasion

One book that opened my eyes to the power of persuasion was *Made to Stick* by Chip Heath and Dan Heath.[3] Ever since it came out in 2007, I've kept coming back to it for its power in public speaking. The Heath brothers studied what makes ideas stick in people's minds, regardless of their validity, and found they contained one or more of these six principles. You can use each one in a speech:

Simplicity: Use a clear, concise message instead of getting lost in the details.

Unexpectedness: Use a surprising quote or statistic that captures people's attention.

Concreteness: Use vivid descriptions that paint a picture in the mind of your audience.

Credibility: Base your quotes or arguments on a credible source, someone the audience knows and respects.

Emotions: Appeal to people's hearts as well as their heads; tap into shared values.

Stories: Tell stories to make the audience feel like they were actually there with you.

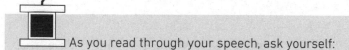 As you read through your speech, ask yourself:

- Does my argument have an appropriate balance of ethos, logos, and pathos?

- Does my argument address the five elements of persuasion? What can I do to create urgency around the issue and give my audience a sense of hope? Do I have an appropriate call to action?

- What persuasive tools will work best?

THE POWER OF STORY

The year was 2012; it was a warm summer day in Washington, DC. I was walking toward a building in Farragut Square, two blocks from the White House. I still remember the business suit I was wearing and the sense of anticipation I felt in my heart. I was about to start a new job in a new city, and I had my whole life ahead of me. What happened next changed everything.

That's the beginning to one of my own personal stories, from a defining moment in my life. Storytelling is one of the most powerful tools you can use to connect with an audience. Our brains react differently to stories than to facts and figures. When you describe smells, sights, or sounds, your audience's brains light up in those sensory areas. Your audience's imaginations actually feel the emotions you describe in your story. Annette Simmons, storytelling expert and author of the book *Whoever Tells the Best Story Wins*, says if a story "changes the emotions of the group, it changes what happens next. Emotion changes behavior." ⊕

Professor Paul Zak, a neuroeconomist at Claremont Graduate University, found that hearing emotional stories releases oxytocin, a chemical that increases trust and empathy in the minds of listeners.[4] If you are speaking to an audience who is skeptical about you, then by hearing a story, they can feel what you feel and relate to you as a person. They start to trust you.

How did your family members form your values? Probably by telling stories about when they were young. My family stories shape who I am and how I perceive myself. Take the story about my grandmother as a young woman taking a bus alone from New York to Florida, or my mother learning to fly a plane while she was nine months pregnant with me. These two stories are part of our family lore and shape my independence and love for travel.

In my experience, the most powerful stories are not the ones where everything goes according to plan: the most powerful stories show a struggle and highlight your failures instead of your strengths. It could be a humorous story that tells the audience you can laugh at yourself, or a story of shame that shows your vulnerability. Through our own failures, audiences see us as human beings and relate to us on a deeper level.

Several years ago, I worked with a group of public school principals in Washington, DC. They were a group of dedicated, driven leaders trying to provide a safe, nurturing learning environment for their students, many of whom came from disadvantaged backgrounds. We brainstormed ways they could win the trust of their students whenever they spoke at school assemblies or even one-on-one. Rather than sharing the stories of their leadership successes, which put them up on a pedestal, these principals instead looked for stories of struggle and loss that made them relatable to their students.

Stories don't have to be overly personal. As a business executive, you can tell a story about when you first started working in your organization and what you learned in that junior role. If you're a sales manager, you can tell your junior salespeople what it was like to open a new office and have to build your own book of business, without any guidance along the way.

And if storytelling is personal, *that's okay.* We are not robots doing business with other robots; we are human beings connecting with other human beings, even if we're talking about finance or policy or supply chain. When we connect on a personal level, we build trust, which leads to better working relationships. If you're pitching a new client, a personal story about how you learned the value of customer service is an incredibly powerful way to say to the client, "I will be here for you."

A caveat: this doesn't mean that the story should be *too* personal. Subjects such as disease or dating or divorce can feel like too much information and can make your audience feel uncomfortable.

Sometimes an international student in my class at Harvard will suggest that using stories is something "you Americans" use. But stories are universal. Using them in a speech or presentation may not be as commonplace in business or politics in your country; but even so, it is still a powerful tool that you can use in your own way. Let's talk about how to find and choose a story.

How to Find a Story

Start with the end in mind. What point are you trying to make? What value are you trying to impart? How do you want your audience to feel? Think about an anecdote from your professional or personal life that illustrates that point. For example, if I were giving a speech about the importance of gender parity in the workplace, I could tell a story about being the only female at a conference.

I picked up a few great exercises from international keynote speaker Olivia Schofield: Make a list of all the pivotal experiences in your life, from childhood through adulthood. Next to each one, write the lesson you learned from it. Or make a list of the important people in your life. Write down how you met them and one story that happened with them. These anecdotes become your story database; the next time you're writing a speech, look through that database to select a story that fits your message.

In *Whoever Tells the Best Story Wins*, Annette Simmons talks about six different types of stories you can use; I highly encourage you to read her book, which walks you through crafting each one.[5] She also uses the following storytelling prompts: tell us about a time you shined; a time you blew it; a mentor; or a book, movie, or current event. Those four prompts reveal rich examples of stories you can share.

How to Choose a Story

When you ask the first of the Three Questions, *Who is your audience?*, you'll know which stories to use. Will your audience relate to stories of perseverance, or failure? Are they more analytical, or emotional? Will your story resonate across borders and across age groups? If the story personally embarrasses you or someone in your audience, it may not be the right story. If you are afraid you'll break down in tears telling the story, it might be too raw to use. If the story references another person, check with that person to make sure you have their permission to use the story.

Don't make up a story: if the purpose of a speech is to build trust with your audience, then you destroy that trust by lying to them. You can make up a *parable*, but be clear that it's not a true story. Similarly, don't use someone else's story as your own. You can reference their story with attribution, but check with them first.

How to Write a Story

I received the following guidance from professor Marshall Ganz at the Harvard Kennedy School, who teaches leadership courses on public narrative and community organizing.[6] ⊕ He explains that a story has a character, a plot, and a moral. Within the plot, there is a challenge, a choice, and an outcome. As you write your story, here are some questions to help you flesh out the story. If you weren't the character in the story, use "you" below to refer to the character.

- Where were you? Focus on one moment in time: set the scene by explaining where you were and what you were doing. Be as descriptive as possible so the audience feels like they were right there with you.

- What happened? What was the challenge that confronted you? Describe what was at stake and how you felt.

- How did you respond? What choice did you make? Your action results in an outcome.

- What was the outcome? Paint a vivid picture of what happened as a result of your action.

- What was the moral? As a result of the story, there is a moral or teaching lesson. Match that moral to a point you are making in your speech.

Mistakes People Make When Telling a Story

1. **They don't tell a story.** They simply list a number of events. A story is something that happened at one point in time.

2. **They skip crucial details.** You were there; you know what happened. But those of us in the audience who weren't there need more details. Make sure your story walks us through what happened without skipping a step—or if you're condensing a long story, make sure the critical transitions are there.

3. **They describe *too many* details.** It's important to provide context in the story, but don't get carried away. Many people reveal so much background that they start to distract from the story itself.

4. **They don't talk about how they *feel*.** The power of a story comes from creating a feeling in the hearts and minds of your audience. And if you don't share how you feel, the audience won't feel anything—about the story or about you.

5. **They don't connect the story to the message.** Some people will tell a story without connecting it to the message of their speech. The story and its moral should be relevant to a point in your speech.

Test your story on others; it's a good way to make sure you feel comfortable telling the story. Sometimes we choose a story without realizing that it feels too personal. If you're telling a story about a family member who passed away after a long battle with disease, and you cannot tell the story without dissolving into tears, then the story might not be ripe yet. It's okay if you show emotion while telling a story—in fact, it's critical—but if it distracts you from the message of the speech, then it might be too personal. Test this out on others before using it in front of an audience.

How to Tell a Story

So you've written a story. How do you use it in your speech? Where do you put it in your speech?

There are three particularly effective ways to use stories: to open your speech, to close your speech, or to illustrate a point. You could do all three, but that depends on the length of your speech and the makeup of your audience. If you're giving a technical presentation or pitch and are concerned that the audience will spend all their time reading the slides instead of looking at you, you can add professional stories to get them off the slides or handouts. Once you start to tell the story, your audience will stop looking at the slides and start connecting with you.

Don't introduce the story. Many people will get up and say, "Good morning, I'm going to tell you a story about something that happened in my life and how it shapes who I am today." Just tell the story. One of my students demonstrated this approach brilliantly when she started her speech with this sentence: "The shooting started at five thirty in the morning."

Don't read the story from notes. The beauty of a story is that you know what you're talking about. You don't need to memorize statistics or background information. Don't worry if it doesn't come out exactly as you practiced—it never will. Trust that, as a result of your practice, you will tell a good story.

Pause after you tell the story, both before and after you reveal the moral. Many times, people will rush through their story and then move to the rest of their speech without giving the audience time to absorb the moral. In the audience, we are experiencing this story for the very first time. We need time to think about what it means for us. Give us time to do that. Make sure your facial expressions and voice match the emotion of the story. If you're talking about a personal tragedy, let your face and tone reflect it.

If you'd like to hear other people's stories, check out TheMoth.org. The Moth's mission is "to promote the art and craft of storytelling and to honor and celebrate the diversity and commonality of human experience." They host live storytelling events around the world and their tagline is *True Stories Told Live.*[7] Some of The Moth's storytellers are famous, but most are not. They are regular people who want to share something that happened to them in their life. I've spoken at one of their storytelling events in Washington, DC, and I'm a devoted listener to their weekly podcast.

Professor Ganz says that "stories, strategically told, can powerfully rouse a sense of urgency; hope; anger; solidarity; and the belief that individuals, acting in concert, can make a difference."[8] Stories help you speak with impact.

Once you've written your speech or presentation, take a step back and ask yourself where you can add a story to illustrate your point. Think through events in your life that have shaped who you are, and turn those into the stories you share going forward.

THE POWER OF HUMOR

Do you think of yourself as a naturally funny person? Are you able to tell jokes that leave people rolling around on the floor in laughter? That's not me. And that's not the kind of humor you need in a speech.

Humor is an incredibly powerful tool. The moment the audience laughs with you, they connect with you. When you use humor, you demonstrate that you're confident enough to laugh and that you don't take yourself too seriously. It can lighten up a difficult subject or situation, calm your nerves, and capture your audience's attention.[9]

When people think of humor, they usually think of telling jokes. They think, "I'm not very good at telling jokes, so I'm not very good at humor." Actually, I don't recommend you tell a joke. There's a particular skill to telling jokes, such as rhythm and pausing. Comedians can work for years on crafting a single joke. Luckily, there are many other ways of using humor in a speech.

Ways of Using Humor in a Speech

Stories. A story with a funny or unexpected outcome is a great use of humor. Maybe it's "the craziest thing to ever happen in our store."

Quote. A humorous quote is a great way to start your speech. I love this quote by George Jessel: "The human brain starts working the moment you are born and never stops until you stand up to speak in public."[10]

Comic image. In the American business world, *Dilbert* comics are a constant source of dry humor. I love the "demotivator" posters sold by www.Despair.com. Just make sure that you have permission to use a particular image.

Situational. Commenting on a shared experience, like the office kitchen or the conference-room air-conditioning, can be a great way to make everyone laugh and remind them that they are all in this together.

I once attended a fabulous (and funny) workshop with humorist and speaker Judy Carter, who spoke for a National Speakers Association DC chapter meeting. Ever since, I have recommended her books and resources on how to use humor in a speech. Her book *The Message of You* has powerful tips and techniques for using humor, as well as being an excellent guide for someone looking to develop their skills as a professional speaker. ⊕

Where to Use Humor

A great place to use humor is in the beginning of the speech—remember Tim the Dairy Farmer telling us to make the audience laugh within the first eight seconds? When introducing myself, I like to say, "My name is Allison Shapira and I'm a recovering opera singer." It captures people's attention because it's unexpected, making them laugh. If no one laughs, then I prepare for a tough audience.

You can use humor right after a difficult subject to lighten up the mood and transition to a new subject. An incredibly effective place to use humor is right after you make a mistake. I once saw a speaker onstage try unsuccessfully to make his slides work. He looked at the audience sheepishly and said, "Live by PowerPoint, die by PowerPoint."

I was once leading a workshop for a US government agency that was simultaneously being broadcast to hundreds of remote workers. I was wearing a lavalier microphone to transmit the audio to those watching remotely. Halfway through my presentation, the microphone stopped working. The audiovisual technician walked up to me while I was in mid-sentence, gave me a handheld microphone, walked behind me, and started fiddling with the microphone receiver clipped to the back of my belt.

How did I respond? I took a minute to pause and breathe, then said to the audience: "I'm going to continue talking and pretend that there *isn't* somebody standing behind me right now playing with my belt." Everybody laughed, eventually the mic issue was resolved, and we kept going. If the audience sees you laugh, then they can relax.

Having talked about the power of using humor, we should also mention the *danger* of using humor. When speaking to people of different nationalities, remember that humor is very cultural. What works in one country may not work in another. My normal opening, "I'm a recovering opera singer," doesn't quite work outside the US, because international audiences don't understand the "recovering" reference. Even in the US, the reference could confuse people. The one time I met one of my musical idols in person, I walked up to her after a concert in Central Park in Manhattan and gushed, "I'm a recovering opera singer, and you have been a huge inspiration!" She took a big step back, looked at me with a worried frown, and asked, "What did you say you were recovering from?"

When using humor, ask yourself if you are making fun of someone. It's okay to laugh at yourself, but not at other people. Think very carefully about whether your humor will come across as prejudicial. Perhaps many years ago it was okay to joke about women worrying about their makeup or clothing. Now, in a professional setting, it demeans the professional value that women bring.

Is it okay to use political humor? By now you're far enough into this book to answer that question: it depends on your audience. Just remember that a closed-door speech is never really closed-door. If your speech is posted online, will the humor still be funny?

If you're uncomfortable using humor, don't force yourself to use it. Find something that you are comfortable with. We've all been in situations where we say something that's supposed to be funny and we hear a wall of silence from our audience. Or, worse yet, a gasp of shock. Try out your humor on someone else to make sure it's funny to others. Practice it, smooth it out, and make sure you don't rush it. It has to feel comfortable to you before you go onstage.

Humor is an incredible tool to make your audience relax and connect with you. Take the time to find humorous styles that work for you, and test them out on others before using them in public.

Think about the audience and venue of your speech. What situational humor can you bring in? Which humorous and relevant stories can you tell that audiences will relate to? Practice them with a friend or colleague to make sure they are funny and appropriate.

CHAPTER 5

Polish the Speech

The Final Steps Most People Neglect

POLISHING THE SPEECH

It's the night before your speech. You're writing late into the night, trying unsuccessfully to create a coherent message while fighting the fear of failure in your mind. You frantically wish you had started writing the speech a week ago instead of waiting until the last minute.

This is the point where you do *not* have time to polish your speech. Yet polishing the speech is one of the most important steps in the speechwriting process. Polishing is what happens when you step back from the text, look at it with a fresh eye, and strategically start to improve the speech. Polishing is best done when you are in a relaxed, creative state—that perfect time of day you have set aside for writing. Here are some things to look for when you polish the speech.

Do you give equal weight to every section? If you have three main points and the first point takes up two-thirds of your speech, make the first point more concise so you spend equal time on all three.

Do you have transitions from one section to the next?
When I'm practicing a speech and can't remember what comes
next, it's usually because I didn't logically transition. For a great
example of transitions in a speech, listen to the annual State of
the Union address by any US president. In the span of about one
hour, the president has to weave together dozens of topics into
one cohesive speech.

Where can you add echo or repetition? Is there one particular phrase in your speech that you can repeat throughout? You
can see it in President Obama's campaign chant, "Yes we can," or
Congressman Bob Inglis's TEDx talk with the echo "You are a
conservative member of Congress." You can watch those videos
at www.speakwithimpactbook.com. ⊕ An echo should reinforce the main message of your speech.

Where can you add personal examples? A powerful way to
make a concept come alive is to tell a story or use a brief anecdote that illustrates your point. Chapter 4 showed you how to
do that effectively.

Where can you add data or statistics? In addition to your
personal story, you can demonstrate how that story is part of a
larger issue by bringing in a statistic.

Where can you build up the audience? Where can you vali-
date their experience? If I'm speaking to employees of one particular company, I will often quote their leadership team to
reinforce the points I'm making. Note: This only works when
the employees have faith in their leadership team!

Where are the potential pitfalls? Sometimes an argument,
quote, or fact sounds reasonable to us, but someone in the audience (or online) could misinterpret it. Read through the speech
or presentation, keeping an eye out for those troublemakers. If

in doubt, talk it through with someone who understands your audience. Look for places where the language doesn't feel natural, and change it so you feel more comfortable. If you go over the speech numerous times and keep pausing in the same place, that's a good sign that you should change the language or the concept.

Exercises You Can Use with Your Audience

As a general rule, I want to capture the audience's attention immediately (within the first eight seconds), and I plan some sort of engagement activity every ten to fifteen minutes. As a trainer, that activity could be a table discussion or a speaking exercise. Even if you're not a trainer, you can still pose a question that your audience members can discuss in groups of two or at their tables.

Trainers know that the more *participants* are talking, the more they are learning. You can include interactivity in a few different places:

At the beginning of a presentation. Help the audience members get to know each other and introduce the topic. For instance, if you are speaking to a group of experts, you could ask them to speak to the person next to them about how they've handled a particular issue, then ask people to volunteer what they discussed.

After making a recommendation. If you are recommending a course of action, you can ask the audience to discuss, in small groups, how they would implement that recommendation and what resistance they would encounter. This helps the audience start to take ownership of the recommendation.

To break up a presentation. If you are about to move to a new point, stopping for discussion is a helpful way to make sure people are following the presentation.

These types of exercises are particularly effective if you work with introverts, where speaking up and commenting in public may not feel comfortable. Regardless of whether they are introverts or extroverts, anyone who experiences speech anxiety might not feel comfortable raising their ideas in public. Small group discussions during your presentation can be an effective way to bring in new ideas that you couldn't otherwise solicit.

> Read through your speech with a critical eye for polish, looking for balance and transitions. Look for ways to even out your content; add repetition, stories, or data; and look for potential pitfalls. Consider ways to add audience interaction, if appropriate.

MAKING YOUR SPEECH MORE CONCISE

One of the most frequently requested topics among our clients and students is how to be concise. In the American business world, conciseness is a valued leadership skill. In other countries, speaking may require winding up to your main points over time; but in the United States, people want you to *get to the point*.

I once had a boss who chaired our weekly staff meetings and was tasked with giving an update on the organization. She had five minutes at the end of the agenda but would often ramble for *up to forty minutes*. We were all ready to get back to work, but this presentation had the effect of reducing our motivation and tiring us out. It did not instill confidence in her leadership!

Among many of my clients, their leadership ability is partly measured by how concise they are when they speak. Our time is valuable and there is important information we need to discuss. No one wants to sit in an endless meeting listening to six lengthy presentations.

The secret to a concise speech is no secret at all: you simply have to be deliberate about it. There is a beautiful quote attributed to the artist Michelangelo. He said, "Every block of stone has a statue inside it, and it is the task of the sculptor to discover it."[1] Your unfinished speech is like a block of marble with a statue waiting to be set free. Once you decide what *does* belong, remove what *doesn't* belong. At every single sentence, ask yourself: "Does this reinforce the main message of the speech? Does it need to be included?" If the answer is no, then get rid of it. The more you say, the less people hear—so make sure that every single word, every single phrase, adds meaning to your speech.

A friend of mine once sent me an anxious text the night before a big speech. He said, "Help! I'm supposed to give the closing remarks at a conference. They asked me to speak for twenty minutes, but I only have fifteen minutes' worth of content. Should I just add some buffer material?" I responded, "In the history of conferences, no audience member has ever complained that the closing remarks were too short. Fifteen minutes is fine." Unless you're a professional speaker getting paid for a ninety-minute keynote, it's okay to end early. If you can say what you need to say in a concise, compelling way, then do it.

Knowing that you should be concise and *being* more concise are two separate things.

Here are some questions to ask that will help you be more concise:

- **What are my three main points?** Do I need to explain them in detail?

- **Do I need every single story or anecdote?** Could I take out one of the examples?

- **Where do I say "and"?** Could I remove the second half of that sentence or phrase?

- **What if I only had half the time to present?** What's essential and what can I discard?

Here are a few more tips for being concise:

- Hand your written speech to a colleague and ask him or her to cut it. It's much easier for someone else to cut your content.

- Ask your colleague to read your speech back to you. When you hear your own language out loud, it's easier for you to see where to cut.

- Create a five-minute version of your speech. If you had to present a simplified version of your presentation, what essential points would you keep? This helps you identify those key points. If your speech was already five minutes, then create a one-minute version.

The more you focus on conciseness, the easier it becomes to be more concise. You'll start to read through material and think, "This isn't relevant," and you'll take it out. This process takes time, discipline, and creativity, as well as respect for your audience. It's not something you can do the night before the speech in a frenzied state; it's something you do with a clear and present mind. Polishing the speech makes the difference between a truly impactful speech and a rambling rant.

Use some of the methods described above to cut out 20 to 50 percent of the content of your speech. Imagine you only had five minutes to present: What key information would you need to keep, and what could you cut out?

ENGAGING YOUR AUDIENCE

How can you engage your audience?

That is one of the biggest questions my clients ask, and it often shows a misunderstanding of the concept. You don't add "audience engagement" to a speech as you would add a story or rhetorical question. Engaging the audience is about capturing their attention, making them *want* to listen to you, and eliciting a positive response—laughter, head-nodding, understanding, agreement, or action. If a speech is a conversation between you and your audience, then *everything you do throughout the speech should engage your audience.* Specifically, you engage people through:

Content: A clear, concise speech with signposts along the way to keep your audience's attention

Delivery: Meaningful eye contact with members of the audience and hand gestures that underscore your words

Energy: A clear voice that demonstrates your passion and conviction and creates energy in the room

Visuals: Painting a picture in your audience's minds, telling a story that lets them feel as if they were in that scenario

Dialogue: Asking a question of the audience, or having them discuss topics with one another

We engage the audience throughout our speech, not at one predetermined time. Everything we do is intended to engage the audience so that we move them to understanding and action. Everything you learn in this book will help you do that.

PRACTICING YOUR SPEECH

Let's say you're a musician or athlete with a big event coming up, where all eyes would be on you and where the future of your career was at stake. Would you make time to practice? I'm betting you would. Practice is essential when playing a musical instrument or a sport, and a speech is no different. A powerful speech can elevate your reputation and career prospects within an organization, or your visibility within your community. So why wouldn't you practice?

Oftentimes, we don't know how to practice and we don't think we have enough time. Some people don't like to practice because they think they'll sound too artificial. But it's not about memorizing a script: it's about smoothing out the rough patches. You can be authentic and polished at the same time.

I'm going to give you seven different ways you can practice, and I'll describe what parts of your speech they will help. It's like using a machine at the gym: each exercise works a different muscle group.

Method 1: Practice Out Loud

Areas of Focus: Language, timing, authenticity

As I mentioned earlier in this chapter, practicing the speech out loud helps you ensure that the language sounds authentic to you and the words feel comfortable to pronounce. You also make sure you keep to your time limit. I use this method as soon as I'm done writing the speech and then again after polishing it.

Method 2: Practice in Front of a Mirror

Areas of Focus: Nonverbal communication

This is the practice method I use the most. I'll stand in front of a mirror and identify three areas behind me to focus my eye contact on (which we'll discuss in Chapter 6). I'll try out different hand gestures and movements to make sure that my movements match my words. I'll practice pausing and making eye contact at the same time to ensure that my main points sink in. And I'll check my posture to make sure I'm standing tall. I do this two or three times before a speech.

Method 3: Practice with a Memo Recorder

Areas of Focus: Vocal variety, enunciation, speed

Practicing with a voice recorder lets you focus only on your voice without getting distracted by body language. When you listen to your voice, ask yourself: Does your energy level match the words? Do you speak slowly and clearly? Does your accent make it difficult for people to understand you? How many filler words do you use? In Chapter 7, I'll provide exercises to help you speak with a powerful voice.

Method 4: Practice with Your Props

Areas of Focus: Visual aids, timing

Using slides in your speech will make you speak for longer than you intend (see Chapter 9 about using slides). If you're preparing to use props—slides, handouts, video, or other visual aids—run through your speech with these tools and time yourself. Also practice setting up the visual aids so that you don't fumble in front of your audience on the day of the speech. If you need an assistant to help you, take steps now to have someone join you the day of the speech.

Method 5: Practice in Front of Others

Areas of Focus: Message, body language, confidence

In every single one of my workshops, people practice their speeches in front of others. It's incredibly valuable to stand in front of a few colleagues, friends, or family members and deliver your speech. Some of my clients will practice their speeches in front of their teenage children, demonstrating that they themselves are not perfect. Practicing in front of others forces you to make eye contact with your audience and receive feedback on your message. If they know the audience and subject of your upcoming speech, then their content-related feedback is very helpful. But if you'll be speaking in front of a diverse audience without a strong background in your area of expertise, practicing in front of people who don't know the field is incredibly valuable. This practice method builds confidence every single time you use it. Use the Feedback Form I've developed at www.speakwithimpactbook.com. ⊕

Method 6: Practice with Your Eyes Closed

Areas of Focus: Nerves, presence, confidence

I learned about mental rehearsal years ago through Toastmasters and have found it to be one of the most powerful practice tools I've ever used. Sit in a comfortable position and close your eyes. Imagine the setting where you will be giving your speech or presentation: the conference or meeting room. Imagine you are excited to speak. Imagine the warm applause as you walk up to the stage or to the front of the room (I know, there probably won't be applause in the meeting room). Pause and breathe, smile, and make eye contact with your audience. Then give your speech—word for word—in your mind. Imagine it going incredibly well. Imagine the warm round of applause as you finish the speech and the mixture of relief and pride you feel walking back to your seat. Imagine someone telling you how impactful your message was for them personally. Visualizations are very powerful; injured athletes use visualizations to keep training even when they can't get onto the field. I use this method while lying in bed the night before the speech. Unfortunately, I sometimes put myself to sleep!

Method 7: Practice with Video

Area of Focus: Everything!

One of the most effective yet feared methods of practice is using video. You can record video on all sorts of devices such as your phone, tablet, or camera. The simpler the tool, the more likely you are to use it. Watching yourself on camera lets you evaluate: your appearance, your body language, your energy level, your message, your pacing—everything! Unfortunately, what we focus on most when watching ourselves on video are the small things only we notice: those few extra pounds or that thinning hair. Acknowledge it, put it aside, and focus on what the audience will see. Mute the sound and just watch the video. Could you guess the subject matter based on your body language? Do your hands match your message? Use this practice tool to evaluate how you come across onstage and write down a few areas to work on based on this video. While many people will shy away from recording a video of themselves, I tell them it's always easier to watch a private video of themselves before they go onstage, as opposed to watching the actual recording of the event when it's later posted online for the world to see!

Finding time to practice

A common complaint among our clients is that they don't have time to practice. Don't have thirty minutes? Ask yourself what the possible outcome of your speech or presentation will be. Will you change people's minds, attitudes, or actions? Isn't that worth displacing another meeting? Especially as your speeches become more high-stakes, you must protect the time you need to be successful. There are hidden minutes all around us if we put down our digital devices and look for them:

- *On an airplane.* This is the perfect place to write, polish, or practice your speech. You can even read it out loud in a low voice. You have minimal distractions.

- *In your car during your commute.* *Note: Keep your eyes on the road and your hands on the wheel.* Talk through the Three Questions in your mind and speak through the main message of your speech. See if you can remember the opening and closing sentences of your speech. Try out different phrases to see which feel most comfortable.

- *Waiting for an appointment.* Sitting in the waiting room for a doctor's appointment or other meeting is a great place to read through the content of your speech.

- *In a taxi on the way to an event.* You can even practice the speech for the driver, since you have a captive audience.

- *First thing in the morning.* Enjoy your morning cup of coffee or tea and let your mind wander to your upcoming speech. Practice mental rehearsal with a warm, comforting beverage in your hand before the rest of the house wakes up. You could also do this right before you go to bed.

What do you do after you practice?

As a result of the different practice methods I use, I no longer need the exact script in front of me. I can reduce the speech to bullet points and bring only those points with me to the speech. I print them out in a large font, often ALL CAPS, with lots of white space, and make the pages single-sided with page numbers at the top. This is my lifeline during the event, a quiet, comforting reminder that if I lose my place, help is right in front of me.

Because of the practice methods I use:

- My language is smoother and more seamless.

- I have fewer filler words because I know what I'm going to say.

- I have more confidence that I know my subject and have a strong sense of purpose.

- My body language is confident and engaging and adds value to the meaning of my words.

- I am able to speak with impact.

In her book *On Speaking Well,* Peggy Noonan says that "[President] Reagan was the most natural speaker in politics, but he was a natural because he practiced so hard."[2]

The more you practice, the more natural you become.

Choose two or three of the above methods to practice your upcoming speech. Reduce the script to bullet points that you can easily refer to when onstage or at the front of a room.

CHAPTER 6

Show What You Mean

The Three Movements That Make Your Speech Come Alive

THINKING ABOUT DELIVERY

You've spent time writing your speech. You've come up with a persuasive message that's written in the language of your audience. You found a moving personal story to reinforce that message and humor that relaxes the audience. And you've included signposts in your speech to guide the audience along the way.

If people even get this far, they usually stop here. They run through the speech in their head and then think the nonverbal delivery will happen naturally, or that it doesn't matter, or that it's part magic and part inspiration. It's none of those.

Delivery is as strategic as the message itself. And to neglect delivery is to do a huge disservice to your message.

When you speak, everything about you is communicating. Your words communicate, but so do your face, your hands, and your attire. In addition, the *sound* of your voice communicates beyond the words. In public speaking, every communication tool you have should say the same thing.

Let's talk about each of these tools and how you can make sure they are in harmony. But first, a caveat. I've taught public speaking on five continents and found that delivery differs in every culture, even within the same organization. For instance, I generally encourage speakers to make eye contact with their audience. But in some cultures, it's inappropriate for women and men to make prolonged eye contact, or for a more junior person to look directly at his or her elders. When speaking within certain cultures, you may need to follow those cultural norms in order to connect with your audience. If you are speaking outside those cultural boundaries, then it's important to know how to adapt your delivery accordingly.

In this book, we're going to look at the best practice that I've found to be most effective for multicultural audiences, but remember that the first question you ask when preparing to speak is, *Who is your audience?* That includes the question *What kind of cultural traditions do you need to respect?*

There are three main types of movement that I focus on when speaking in public, and I call them the Three Movements:

1. Eye Contact

2. Body Language

3. Voice

1. EYE CONTACT

The employees of one organization we worked with gave frequent client presentations and, in our workshops, we would conduct role-plays simulating those presentations. I remember one person who would present with his eyes fixed firmly on the table in front of him instead of looking at his clients. He was presenting valuable market research, yet his lack of eye contact undermined the credibility of that research.

A great speech or presentation should feel like a conversation between you and every single member of the audience. After the speech, each audience member should think, "Wow, I felt like she was speaking directly to me."

Imagine you're meeting someone for the first time at a networking event. You smile and shake hands with this new person, but he doesn't look you in the eye: he looks down at his shoes or above your head or at someone else in the room. How does that make you feel? We've all experienced this kind of awkward networking situation, and sometimes we've been that person looking away, whether out of nerves, a lack of confidence, or a lack of respect for others.

When you don't make eye contact with your audience, you appear nervous, unsure of yourself, unprepared, or distracted. There are exceptions, of course. Sometimes with a very personal story, you might prefer to look down rather than at your audience. Sometimes you might look thoughtfully to the side while thinking about a certain point. And sometimes you have to read from a script due to the formality of the occasion.

But as a general rule, if you want to influence people, you have to connect with them on a personal level. And one of the most basic ways in which we connect with other human beings is through eye contact.[1] When you look at one person at a time during a speech, you connect with each one as an individual.

There are certain times when it's critical to make eye contact.

When you state your name. It's a declaration of your own sense of confidence in yourself, akin to saying, "I believe in myself and my right to be standing in front of you at this moment."

When you thank people. I once observed a senior leader thank her team for their wonderful work while looking down at her notes, making the praise sound insincere and hollow. When you thank people, look at them.

When you ask a question. If you want your audience to answer a question, make eye contact to show that the question is directed toward them.

When you state a main point. Your main points are the essential linchpins in your speech. Tee them up by pausing, making eye contact, speaking the points slowly and clearly, and then pausing again. That delivery brings home your message.

When you make a request. If your speech includes a call to action, make eye contact. Reinforce that personal connection when you ask people to do something.

Where do people tend to look instead?

They look down at their script, at the floor, or—if seated at a conference table—at the center of the table. People also tend to look above the heads of their audience or off to the side. They do this most often when they are thinking, their eyes sliding up and to the side. And while it's okay to do this every once in a while, remember that when you look away from the audience, you create a barrier. Eye contact reduces that barrier. You can look away to think and gather your thoughts, but come back to the audience to actually speak.

How do you make meaningful eye contact?

My colleague and public speaking expert Trudi Bresner recommends making eye contact with one person while completing a full thought. Then, choose another person to make eye contact with and complete a full thought. Continue throughout the speech. Do you make eye contact with every person? It depends on the size of the audience. Know who the major decision-makers are and look at them when making a key point—but don't speak *only* to the decision-makers. As you can imagine, staring at any one person for too long will make them feel uncomfortable. In fact, during our workshops, I might do that on purpose just to make a point. Once the person starts to squirm uncomfortably in his or her chair, I highlight the fact that excessive eye contact can alienate someone in your audience.

Using this method of eye contact forces you to slow down and truly connect with each person. It also helps you calm down and be fully present. If you sweep your eyes back and forth across the room, you absorb too much information and can get overwhelmed by everyone looking at you.

In fact, one challenge when making eye contact is that you are observing your audience as much as they are observing you. You start to pick up on cues. You notice the man sitting *right up front* is having an intense texting conversation. Or the woman sitting to the side is staring off into the distance. Or someone in the back has his arms crossed with a big frown on his face. We tend to overanalyze these signals.

I remember the first professional speech I ever gave. I was speaking to a youth group in Worcester, Massachusetts, about the Israeli-Palestinian conflict. This was in 2002, during the time of the second Intifada, and I was trying to explain a complicated and constantly evolving crisis that I was still becoming familiar with myself.

There was a man sitting in the back of the room. He was leaning back in his chair with his arms and legs crossed and a huge frown dividing his face. Throughout the speech, my mind kept racing. *Why is he frowning? Are my facts accurate? Do I even know what I'm talking about? I'm a fraud!* At the end of the speech, the man approached me. My heart started beating loudly and my mouth went dry. I started preparing for the litany of arguments he would use to pick apart my speech. I took a nervous breath, steadied myself, and smiled awkwardly. The man leaned in, and his brow furrowed even more. He took my hand and gave it a strong, powerful handshake. Keeping that same frown, he said to me: "Young lady, that was a fantastic speech!"

A wave of relief washed over me, followed by confusion. *I spent the entire speech thinking that this person hated it, and it turns out he loved the speech?* I vowed at that moment not to get too carried away in the future by someone's reaction.

Just as a speaker communicates to the audience through her body language, the audience also communicates with us, whether intentionally or not. Crossed arms could mean the room is cold. A frown could come from a fight he had with his kids that morning. A head buried deep in a cell phone could be avoiding a last-minute press disaster. None of that is your fault—don't let it distract you from your speech.

What if you really must read from notes? Maybe the speechwriter at your company gave you the remarks at the last minute. Maybe the public affairs team drafted talking points and you need to stick to the script during a crisis. I've observed people very effectively read from a script. They pause to raise their eyes up to the audience at the end of a sentence, connecting with one person at a time (I learned that technique from speechwriter Stephen Krupin, whom I referenced in Chapter 3). They let their voice and energy convey the same strength and passion as if they were having a conversation. It takes some practice, but you can read effectively and still connect with your audience. ⊕

When you're speaking on the phone, you may think that eye contact doesn't matter, but be careful. On the phone, you have a tendency to multitask by looking at your emails or phone messages. Believe me, we can sense when someone is distracted when they are speaking to us. When presenting over the phone, either make eye contact with your notes or look at a neutral part of the room so that you can stay focused on the material.

Once you've finished writing your speech, stand in front of a mirror. Look back at your reflection and choose three or four items behind you that will serve as people. Take turns speaking to each one of them for a full phrase, then move on to another. Then, gather a few friends or colleagues; give your speech to them and focus solely on eye contact. Look at each person for a full thought, then move on. You'll start to develop a natural rhythm.

2. BODY LANGUAGE

How do you walk into a room? How do you stand or sit when speaking? Do you throw your shoulders back and stand tall, or do you slouch and fold your arms across your chest protectively? Do you keep your feet firmly planted on the floor, or do you cross one leg over the other? These movements are among the first things people notice about you.

Let's talk about your smile.

Your smile is one of the most disarming tools you have. You can use it to reduce stress, defuse anger, and provide comfort to your audience. You can use it to show confidence, enthusiasm, and happiness. The act of smiling makes your brain release hormones like dopamine and serotonin, making you feel happier and less stressed.[2] I'm not talking about forcing a smile; I'm talking about letting yourself smile.

Unfortunately, sometimes people forget to smile. They stand in front of an audience and say "I'm really happy to be here" with their eyes dead and their face slack. It's usually their nerves holding them back, or perhaps they think in a business setting it's inappropriate to smile. Conversely, some people smile inappropriately. You can't propose painful budget cuts with a big grin on your face. Your facial expressions should match your words.

When I was a teenager, I hated my smile. In pictures, it always looked stilted and false, like I was trying too hard. Having braces didn't help either. But I had just started performing, and people were taking my picture. So one day I stood in front of a mirror and practiced my smile. Back then, we didn't have smartphones (or any kind of cell phones) to help us, but these days you can easily take your own photos and determine what kind of smile works best.

A smile is universal. A few years ago, I was leading workshops in the Palestinian Territories on behalf of the US State Department. One day, I gave a presentation for a large group of students at Al-Najah University in Nablus. The room was packed with students. I spoke in English, and my remarks were simultaneously interpreted into

Arabic. In preparation, I had spent a great deal of time dividing my suggestions into what was universal and what was culturally specific in public speaking, and I decided to ask the students, what they thought.

During the workshop, I asked the students, "What do *you* think is important when giving a speech?" A woman in the back of the room raised her hand so we could pass her a microphone. She was wearing a white *niqab* that covered her face and body so I could only see her eyes. She took the microphone and stood up. She faced me and said, calmly and confidently in English, "It's very important to smile when you are speaking in public!" I paused, thrown off by the fact that we couldn't see her face but still she wanted us to smile. Finally, I said, "Yes; even if we can't see your face, we can hear your smile," to which she responded enthusiastically: "Yes! I'm smiling! I'm smiling!" We all appreciate the power of a smile.

Speaking over the phone, a smile is *crucial*. It warms your voice and makes you sound more confident. If you spend a lot of time on the phone with clients, colleagues, or volunteers, smile while you're speaking. Don't believe me? Ask someone to repeat the same two sentences (once without smiling, once smiling) while you listen with your eyes closed. You will hear the difference.

There are other things you can do with your face besides smile. You can furrow your eyebrows and then relax your forehead; you can look cynical or sarcastic. The words and the tone of the speech will dictate your facial expressions. You have a naturally expressive face. Let yourself use it when you are in front of an audience.

What do you do with your hands?

One of the most frequently asked questions I get about delivery is what to do with your hands. Do you leave them at your sides? How much movement is too much? There is no one magical movement you should make with your hands. It all depends on the message and context of your speech. Your hand gestures should reinforce your words.

Look through your speech and identify your main points. Are you talking about size, distance, or time? Let your hands show those concepts. Are there specific words that are crucial to your argument? Let your hands reinforce them with a sweeping gesture.

There are two kinds of body language: nervous and intentional. Nervous body language comprises all those unintentional ticks: wringing our hands while we talk, playing with our rings, taking our glasses on and off when we don't need to, or pacing around the room. These movements literally tell the audience that we are nervous, broadcasting our discomfort across the room.

Intentional body language is different; it emphasizes your points and highlights your message. It should *add* to your words instead of distracting from them. When you move your hands, keep your fingers closed, as opposed to spreading them out. Instead of always using the same repetitive features, make sure each gesture matches your words. Every time you use your hands, use them with intention and purpose.

I like to find a "home base," a place I can keep my hands most of the time so I don't have to think about it. I keep my arms comfortably bent at a 90-degree angle, with my hands apart, relaxed. Then I can gesture with my hands when needed, and return them to home base. I don't have to think about it; it becomes automatic. I can also simply leave my hands at my sides; you can see a video I made on this subject at www.speakwithimpactbook.com. ⊕

A few years back, I was teaching in a leadership development program with a group of other instructors. One of the instructors participated in my public speaking workshop. He came up to me a few days later and told me: "Remember when you said to practice body language in front of a mirror? Well, I saw a picture of us standing in front of the room on the first day of this program. You had your arms relaxed at your sides, and mine were stiff and folded in a fig-leaf position. You looked so comfortable and I looked so awkward! So I practiced different hand gestures, trying to find that 'home base' you talked about. I thought, 'This is weird; it's never going to look good.' Then I walked over to the mirror and tried it out, and it looked so natural! Now I have a more comfortable place to keep my hands." Practice it and it will become natural.

Finally, let's talk about your feet.

Look through your speech to see where you talk about distance or time. Move around the room when you go from one point in time to the next. As a general rule, I like to walk around during transitions and then pause to make a point. Is your speech outline chronological? Start on one side of the room and then walk to the other as your argument progresses. If you want to refer back to something from an earlier time, walk back to that place on the stage.

Walking around the room is a great way to engage the audience. If you see people on their phones or having side conversations, you can casually walk closer to them while speaking; your presence will make them pay attention. No one wants to get caught by the teacher for talking in class!

How much should you walk around? It depends on the size of the room or stage. The larger the stage, the larger the movements can be. In a small conference room, you will have a much smaller area to work with. What you don't want to do is rock back and forth or pace back and forth—these are nervous body movements that distract the audience and broadcast your nervousness. Instead, stand tall with your weight on both feet and your shoulders back.

How do you present while seated? You might be sitting across a conference table from clients, or on a videoconference with people on the other side of the world. In these cases, your body language is just as important. Your hand gestures can still reinforce your message; and on video, your smile is more important than ever because the camera is pulling your facial expression down. Keep a half-smile on your face, which makes you look interested and attentive. In Chapter 9, we'll specifically address virtual presentations.

While seated, sit tall in your chair instead of slumping. Lean in slightly, so you shorten the distance between you and your audience. Make eye contact with everyone around the table and make sure you don't turn your back to anyone. Keep your feet flat on the floor so you can ground yourself.

At this point, you might worry that you need to "act out" your speech. Remember that it doesn't need to be perfect. My goal is to help you come up with natural gestures that add to your message and help you get rid of the nervous movements that are distracting from your authority and credibility.

Record a practice video of your speech; watch it with the sound off. From your facial expressions and movements, can you tell the emotion of your speech? Now try giving the speech and acting it out as if you were in front of small children. Don't worry—I don't want you to actually do this in front of an audience; but it will warm up your body and remind you of what you are capable of doing. Then you can try out more natural body language in front of a mirror. Remember I talked about practicing your smile in front of a mirror? Now it's time to practice your hand gestures in front of the mirror. Try out different movements and make them purposeful and firm.

3. VOICE

As a former opera singer, the voice is my favorite subject in public speaking. During my musical training, I spent years learning the power of the human voice to connect with and move an audience. It's one of the *most* important and *least* understood areas for public speakers, and it can make the difference between a powerful and a powerless speech.

Take a minute and think of someone with a truly powerful voice. What is it that makes a strong voice? Maybe it's the pitch—he has a deep voice that carries across the room. Maybe it's the energy—she sounds like she cares about her subject.

It's easy to recognize when someone has a strong voice but harder to actually affect the sound of your own voice. People will receive feedback from their peers or bosses that their voice is too high or too low, without ever learning what they can do to change it. In fact, most people I work with *hate* the sound of their voice. When they hear their voice on a video during our workshops, they cringe. Our voice sounds different to others than it does to us. When you speak, you hear your voice in two concurrent ways: coming in through your ears and resonating inside your head. When you hear it played back to you, you're only hearing it through your ears. Your voice will *always* sound different on a recording than when you speak live.

However, there is a lot you can do to improve the sound of your voice. First, let me explain why it's important.

How many times have you doubted someone's sincerity based on their tone of voice? Read the following sentence out loud seven times, each time emphasizing a different word: "I didn't know he would be there." With each word you emphasize, the meaning of the sentence completely changes. That's how important voice and emphasis are to a speech. Repeat the word "Really?" over and over again, each time with a different emotion: excitement, curiosity, skepticism, and annoyance. It will have a different meaning each time.

Most of us are not intentional about using our voice. Or worse: our nerves get the better of us and reduce our voice to a dry, monotonous tone. But that's not how you normally speak. When you have a regular conversation, your voice naturally rises and falls, depending on your accent. You emphasize certain words to make a point. Your emotions color the tone and we can tell if you are happy or sad, nervous or confident.[3] In fact, a study by Michael Kraus of Yale's School of Management found that people were more accurately able to hear the emotion in people's voices when simply listening to a recording of a conversation, as opposed to both watching *and* hearing the conversation.[4]

Your voice is incredibly expressive when you vent to your spouse about something that happened at work or tell your friends about a recent vacation. And yet, when you stand up to give a presentation, all that color and richness falls away and you sound like a lifeless robot. Why? I've observed a few different factors that reduce the fullness of your voice:

Your nerves do it. When you get nervous, your breathing becomes shallow and your throat constricts, taking all the energy out of your voice. As a singer, I could always hear the tremor in my voice when I was nervous. In the next chapter, I'll show you how to calm your nerves so that your voice can ring loud and clear.

You might think that's how you're supposed to speak. Many of us have the idea that it's unprofessional to show emotion in a speech. The amount of emotion you show certainly depends on the context and on the audience, but there's nothing unprofessional about making the words come alive through your voice.

You may think, That's just the way I sound! But you don't have to. We pick up many things from others, from regional accents to filler words. We can change them if we want to. I'll show you how.

There are other factors in play, such as the microphone or the acoustics in the room. Through the techniques I teach you, you'll be able to overcome those factors and enhance the sound of your voice.

And as if those weren't enough, there is fascinating research correlating the pitch of your voice to your business success. A Duke University study of male CEOs found that CEOs with a deeper voice, on average, made more money than those with higher voices.[5] In another study that manipulated the pitch of male and female voices, both male and female participants preferred leaders with deeper voices.[6]

I know what you're thinking. *So I need to consciously lower the sound of my voice to be more successful?* No, it's not about forcing your voice into a lower register. It's about learning to harness the power of your voice to make it rich and resonant—which will in turn make it naturally a little lower.

I also want to make a point about gender and voice. When Margaret Thatcher became prime minister of the United Kingdom, she consciously worked on the sound of her voice.[7] The effect was that her soft-spoken, singsong voice became lower and deeper. You can hear this for yourself by going to www.speakwithimpactbook.com. ⊕ When I showed Margaret Thatcher's before/after video to my class of graduate students at the Harvard Kennedy School, there was a mixed reaction. A man commented that he liked Thatcher's original voice because "it sounded softer and more feminine."A woman shot back: "Well, the second voice is how I want my prime minister to sound." Cultural expectations can shape our perceptions of tone and power.

So how do you harness the power of your voice when you speak? The next chapter will go into this process in depth because the breathing technique you use is key to projecting your voice.

In addition, your tone of voice reflects how you feel about your subject—and about yourself. Do you care about your subject? Are you proud of the work you do? Do you feel confident in your ability to speak about this issue? Whether you answer "yes" or "no" to those questions will have an effect on the way your voice sounds.

When my team and I work with people on their voice, we start with breathing and confidence-building techniques. We focus on the third of the Three Questions—*Why you?*—because the answer to that question builds your confidence in yourself and your subject. The last section of Chapter 7 includes additional tools such as the Core Value Statement that will build your confidence. Working from the inside out, internal confidence affects your external voice.

Your voice should match the words you use. Do you use numbers to illustrate a daunting challenge your company faces? Let your voice slow down to emphasize the scale of the problem. Do you talk about an injustice in your country? Let your voice show your outrage. Do you include a personal story to demonstrate your connection to the audience? Let your voice show vulnerability. Your voice is incredibly expressive; use it to add meaning to your words. Otherwise, it will undermine your message and undermine your impact.

You know how to do this naturally, but in professional life you may have learned to withhold it for the reasons I mentioned above. Here are a few exercises to let it out:

Radio voice. Imagine giving your speech on the radio where no one can see your facial expressions. You have to reach your audience solely through the sound of your voice. Read your speech out loud, recording yourself with the memo recorder of your phone. Play it back, and you will hear yourself speak more slowly and intentionally.

Speaking to children. When you speak to young children, your voice is naturally more expressive than when you speak to adults. With children, you don't have to act like a professional, and you can make your voice silly and emotional. Read your speech out loud as if you were reading a story to young children while using the exact language of the speech. You'll notice your voice becomes much slower and more expressive.

Practice different emotions. Make a list of different feelings: anger, joy, boredom, excitement. Read sections of your speech out loud and try out different emotions. Record them all on your phone and listen back. Which voice best matches the emotion of your speech? Keep that emotion in mind as you give the speech.

Emphasize every word. Especially if you tend to rush or mumble, concentrate on pronouncing every single word. Speak slowly and clearly and build a new natural rhythm for yourself. One woman I worked with was not a native English speaker but needed to pitch to her clients in English. After working on her pacing and enunciation, she was able to create a new rhythm when she spoke. At the very next meeting with a client, she was able to close the deal. She later told me that she believed her slower pace helped her listen more to the client and address his questions, leading to greater understanding and trust.

Everyone responds to these exercises in different ways, so choose one that works best for you. And don't worry, I don't want you to get in front of an audience and actually sound like you are reading to children. These exercises unlock your full voice and remind you what you are capable of producing.

OVERCOMING COMMON TRAPS: FILLERS, MINIMIZERS, UPTALK, AND VOCAL FRY

Filler Words

Vocal disfluencies, commonly described as filler words, are a common pet peeve in public speaking. Some people disparage them as weak and hesitant, and others defend them as authentic and genuine. I like to follow the philosophy of Robert L. Finder, Jr., author of *The Financial Professional's Guide to Communication*, who likens filler words to ants at a picnic. He writes, "A single ant won't ruin your picnic, but then again, when did you see just a single ant at a picnic?"[8]

Used sparingly, there's nothing wrong with filler words. The problem is when you use them excessively and they detract from your confidence and credibility. If you make a strong argument but use *ah, ah*, repeatedly, it sounds like you're making up the message as you go along. If every speech or presentation is an opportunity to exercise leadership, it won't sound inspiring if every other word is a filler.

What are the most common filler words? We all know about *um, ah*, and *like*. Some others I hear are: *so* (to start sentences), *right?* (to end sentences), *kind of* and *sort of* (in the middle of sentences). People in the same organization tend to use the same filler words. In one company, everyone used the words "*basically*" or "*at the end of the day.*" Professor Tim Murphey of Kanda University of International

Studies says that picking up language from those around us—what he calls linguistic contagion—is a normal form of language acquisition and learning.[9] We can pick up positive, powerful speaking habits by observing and speaking with others. The flip side is that we can also pick up negative habits like filler words that reduce our impact and credibility.

Every language has its own filler words, placeholders as people think about the next thing they want to say: French: *euh,* Spanish: *e,* Italian: *cioè,* Hebrew: *ke'ilu,* Arabic: *ya'ani.*

Minimizers

In addition to filler words, there are minimizers, which play a similar role. Certain phrases and words minimize the impact of your speech by downplaying what you say. *Maybe this is irrelevant, but . . . I may be way off base here, but . . .* or single words, like *sorry* or *just: I just think that we might want to take another look at that issue . . . Sorry, but I just want to say . . ."* *Just* is my personal pet peeve because it trivializes what you say next.

There's a lot of attention focused on women using excessive minimizers, with articles calling on women to stop using them and counter-articles calling on society to stop telling women what to do. ⊕ For women working in mostly male environments, minimizers become especially dangerous because many women already feel like they are fighting to be taken seriously in that environment; by using minimizers, they devalue the power of their ideas. In my experience hearing minimizers in both men and women, the cause is either linguistic contagion (everyone's doing it) or a lack of confidence. Neither men nor women should devalue the power of their ideas.

Sometimes, however, minimizers are intentional. In one workshop, participants pushed back when I tried to minimize their minimizers. They said, "Given the politics of our organization, we have to use these words when providing feedback to leadership." In that case, the use of minimizers becomes strategic. You decide when and if to use them—but be intentional about it.

How do you reduce the frequency of both fillers and minimizers? There are a few techniques I use.

Pause and Breathe. In between sentences, physically close your mouth and breathe in and out through your nose. You can't say a filler word if your mouth is closed!

Knock on the Table. In coaching sessions, I might knock on the table every time I hear a filler word. Yes, it's incredibly distracting for about ten minutes, but then the fillers naturally fall away. The speaker learns to *pause and breathe* instead of using a filler and sounds more thoughtful. You can do the same thing with a practice buddy.

Use an App. Speak out loud using an app like Ummo to count your fillers. Ummo will make a chiming noise each time it hears you use the fillers, which gives you immediate feedback. When you hear the filler, *pause and breathe* and repeat the sentence. Note: Only use this app while practicing, not during an actual speech. ⊕

One Minute of **Ums.** Here's an exercise from my colleague Trudi Bresner that is both effective and fun. Record yourself for one full minute speaking about a topic (perhaps your upcoming vacation) with as many fillers as you can. Go ahead, let them all out. This will make you more conscious of what they sound and feel like. Then, record yourself for one full minute speaking about the same topic *without using a single filler*. Practice with someone else and have them force you to start over when you use a filler. (This will teach you how to suppress them and *pause and breathe* instead.) You will sound much more purposeful and thoughtful.

Focus on reducing these fillers and minimizers in the *practice* stage, not when you actually give your speech. If you remove them in practice, they will start to go away during the speech itself. I once observed one of my clients' internal business reviews with the head of his organization. He caught himself using a filler and instinctively knocked on the table as we had done in our sessions. He paused, said, "That was an inside joke," and quickly moved on. Luckily, I had also worked with the head of the organization, so she also knew our technique! Don't think about it while you're actually presenting.

Uptalk

Uptalk happens when your tone rises at the end of a declarative sentence, making it sound like a question instead of a statement. It's also known as high rising terminal or rising inflection. You often hear it when people introduce themselves: "My name is Allison Shapira?" Visit www.speakwithimpactbook.com to hear an example of uptalk. ⊕

Imagine you're pitching an idea to an investor or prospect. You're an expert in your field and have researched your subject thoroughly. You believe strongly in the value of your work. But then you say, "We have thirty years of experience in this area?" or, "We believe this is the best solution to your problem?" When you let your voice rise into a question, you undermine the entire message.

Around the world, uptalk can be a natural part of the accent. In fact, when my team and I teach public speaking outside the United States, we rarely discuss this subject. But in an English-speaking context in the US, the UK, and elsewhere, uptalk can come across as a lack of certainty or a lack of confidence. You sound like you're questioning your own credibility.

People will also use it when they are unsure of their answer. Instead of stating a fact with certainty, they let the uptalk reveal their uncertainty. They will also use it when they are unsure of their social position within the group. A younger professional will use it more often when he's unsure of his right to speak up.

Some people use uptalk to sound more collaborative, akin to asking, "Are you with me?" at the end of each sentence. I hear it a lot among women, especially given our socialization to "play well with others." Either consciously or unconsciously, we are trying to make sure people agree with us. As with filler words, we pick it up from others. I once coached a Turkish woman to help her adapt to working in an American corporation. When I asked her about her constant use of uptalk, she said, "Well, that's the way all the women in my office sound."

I hear both men and women use uptalk and believe it can be dangerous to your credibility regardless of your gender—although it can be even more damaging if you are one of the few women in a room.

Every time you speak, you have an opportunity to build a relationship of trust with your audience. When you sound like you're questioning yourself, you reduce the audience's trust in you.

How do you reduce uptalk? Record yourself and listen to your tone of voice. Does your voice rise at the end of sentences even when they are not questions? Ask yourself if it's due to a regional accent, and ask yourself how it will sound to an English-speaking audience.

Practice ending your sentences like you are coming down a set of steps, says voice coach Helen Moses. Record yourself and listen to the difference.

When you practice your speech or presentation, make a conscious effort to reduce uptalk in your introduction, your main points, and your conclusion—the most critical parts of your speech—so you don't introduce uncertainty. It's absolutely fine to introduce doubt into your speech when discussing numerous sides to a complex issue. Indeed, it shows your ability to look holistically at an issue. However, when you make a statement on something about which you feel strongly, don't make it sound like a question.

Vocal Fry

Vocal fry happens when you squeeze your vocal cartilage together, making the vocal cords flutter instead of vibrate smoothly. This produces a low, gravelly sound. If you haven't heard vocal fry before, take a minute and go to www.speakwithimpactbook.com so you can recognize the concept. ⊕ Some people speak with vocal fry constantly while others use it only sparingly; I can turn it on and off—on demand—in order to demonstrate what it is.

Why do we do it? Sometimes we are lazy in our breathing, especially at the ends of our sentences. Sometimes there has been physical damage to our vocal cords, which produces it. Oftentimes, we pick it up from others, especially when pop culture stars like Kim Kardashian or musicians like Katy Perry use it. But it's not only women: men use it, too. And while female on-air journalists may get hate mail from using it, male journalists use it as well.[10]

What's the effect on our listeners? It depends on your audience. Since it's more common in young people, a younger audience probably won't even notice it. But if your audience is more mature, it can affect your credibility.

A 2014 study by researchers at Duke University and the University of Miami found that vocal fry had negative repercussions in the job market that disproportionally affected women more than men. "Relative to a normal speaking voice, young adult female voices exhibiting vocal fry are perceived as less competent, less educated, less trustworthy, less attractive, and less hirable."[11] Unfortunately, this is another example where something both men and women do is perceived as more hurtful to women.

If you have something powerful to say, let your voice convey that power. If you reduce your voice to a croak and let it drop off at the end of a sentence, you're taking the air out of your words.

In the next chapter, I'll show you how breathing will reduce vocal fry.

We've covered some critical ground in this chapter to help you harness the power of your voice, but no discussion on voice is complete without understanding how to breathe. Let's dive right into the next chapter to understand how you can use breathing to calm your nerves and power your voice.

CHAPTER 7

Pause and Breathe

Calm Your Nerves and Strengthen Your Voice

OVERCOMING SPEECH ANXIETY

Do you ever get nervous before a speech or presentation? Even if you're not afraid of public speaking, I'm betting you still get butterflies in your stomach before you speak. Most people (myself included) get nervous before a speech, presentation, or important meeting. How nervous you get depends on a lot of factors, such as how often you speak in public, how well you know the subject, and how important the occasion.

In my travels, I encounter this fear again and again. I could be in the Middle East, Asia, Africa, Europe, or Latin America, and the questions will be the same: How do I calm my nerves?

Why do we have this widespread, universal fear of public speaking? Some theories say the reason is primal. Millions of years ago, banding together in communities protected us from predators and allowed us to thrive. Glenn Croston, author of *The Real Story of Risk*, says, "When faced with standing up in front of a group, we break into a sweat because we are afraid of rejection. And at a primal level, the fear is so great because we are not merely afraid of being embarrassed, or judged. We are afraid of being rejected from the social group, ostracized and left to defend ourselves all on our own. We fear ostracism still so much today it seems, fearing it more than death, because not so long ago getting kicked out of the group probably really was a death sentence."[1]

Psychologist and speaker Guy Winch explains, "The same areas of the brain become activated when we experience rejection as when we experience physical pain," and we remember social pain much more vividly than physical pain.[2] That's why, twenty years later, we still cringe when remembering that embarrassing thing we said or did in public.

Luckily, there is much you can do to calm your nerves. When I work with clients, I try to identify the exact cause of their anxiety to see if we can address it directly. I'll use the words *anxiety, nerves,* and *fear* in this section, but if you suffer from severe anxiety or anxiety disorders, then it's a good idea to consult a mental health professional.

We feel anxiety physically as well as emotionally. Our heart races, our hands shake, and some of us blush or develop nervous tells. In Chapter 8, I'll share my pre-speech ritual to help you reduce those physical feelings of anxiety. Meditation and mindfulness provide incredibly powerful tools to center your mind, and deep breathing will do wonders to calm your nerves.

Here are some common causes of public speaking anxiety along with my solutions for how to handle them. Once you identify the source, you can look at specific, practical ways to calm your anxious feelings. Even after isolating all the below factors, you will still be nervous, and that's normal. Fear and excitement *both* produce adrenaline, so reframing your nerves as excitement helps you use that same hormone in a productive way.

Lack of confidence. If you don't believe you have anything of value to say, then you will probably avoid public speaking. *Why would anyone listen to me?* Go back to the Three Questions in Chapter 2 and remind yourself of your *Why you?* Find an authentic passion or interest related to the subject, and let that boost your confidence. Later in this chapter, do the Core Value Statement and read that statement out loud before every speech.

Not enough time to prepare. This is one of the most common reasons people are uncomfortable speaking in public: they didn't have enough time to prepare, or they didn't prepare the right way. Look at Chapter 3 about preparing a speech and, specifically, how to prepare a speech in thirty minutes. It's not about spending endless time preparing; it's about having a tried-and-true process for using the time you have effectively.

Not enough knowledge of the subject. This is a big factor when speaking to people who know more than you. You worry that your audience will pick apart your argument or think you don't know what you're talking about. You could do research and shore up your knowledge, you could limit the scope of your speech, or you could plan ways to bring your expert audience into the speech. For instance, you can ask the audience: "Since we have so many experts in the room, what have you found to be successful?"

Negative experiences or feedback. Maybe you had a traumatic speaking experience in middle school, or perhaps a teacher or parent discouraged you early on. Those early (or even recent) negative experiences can stay with us and color the way we look at the world. Talk through those experiences with a coach, friend, or therapist. By speaking about them out loud, you start to recognize that they describe a past experience, but they don't define who you are. Ask yourself *Why you?* and look ahead at the Core Value Statement to find your confidence.

Negative work environment. If you work in a toxic environment where speaking up means being criticized by your boss or peers, you might fear public speaking. It will feel risky to speak up because it *is* risky. Determine who your allies are within your organization or your community. Who will stand up for your work? Practice your speech with that person and get their feedback on how to phrase your language in a way your colleagues will relate to. That person can then publicly praise your speech or presentation as a way to demonstrate public support for your position.

Don't like being the center of attention. Introverts will tell me they are not afraid of speaking, but they don't like to be the center of attention. In that case, reframe the purpose of the speech. Rather than thinking of the speech as being about *you*, think of the speech as an opportunity to highlight an important issue. You are no longer the center of attention, *your idea* is the center of attention. When he spoke at the Sixth & I Historic Synagogue in Washington, DC, Rabbi Scott Perlo said it beautifully: "If you carry a message of hope and healing, your greatest responsibility is to get out of the way and let the message work its way through you."

Lack of control. When you give a speech or presentation, there are things you can't control: the room's audiovisual, the audience's reaction, and (sometimes) your own imagination. There are two solutions that you can implement simultaneously. First, control all the variables that you can. What if the AV doesn't work? Get there early and make sure you have a technician present. What if there's traffic? Plan that into your schedule. For each "What if?" worry, find a solution. Concurrently, recognize that *you can't control everything*. Even if you test the AV beforehand, it could still stop working. Things will still go wrong, so identify ways to calmly deal with them. If the audience sees you as cool and collected even when there's a problem, you retain your credibility as a speaker.

Fear of your mind going blank. I often hear people say they are afraid they'll forget the words, or that their mind will go blank in front of the audience. It's happened to me as well. Before you go onstage, ask yourself *Why you?* to refocus your attention on your sense of purpose instead of on your nerves.

Bring notes or an outline; I use that for every single speech or presentation. I might not look at the notes, but the fact I have them calms my fear. If you need to, write out the first and last sentences. Print your notes in a large font with plenty of white space and make the paper single-sided so you can easily move from one page to the next. There's also fascinating research showing that chewing gum before a speech or test improves immediate word recall. Just remember to spit out the gum before you go onstage![3]

Don't do it often enough. It's understandable that if you don't speak in public often, you won't feel comfortable doing it. The solution is to speak up more! There are so many opportunities for you to speak. I have found Toastmasters clubs to be the best value for practicing your public speaking in a safe, nurturing environment. Refer back to Chapter 1 to find more places to speak.

Don't know how to do it. Many people fear public speaking because they simply don't know how to do it. It's as if you had to play a new musical instrument in front of a group of peers for the first time. Of course you'd be nervous! The solution is: learn. Read this book. Take a course. Work with a coach. Public speaking is a skill, and the more you build this skill, the more you build your confidence and overcome your fear.

Talk. Talk through your public speaking fears with a friend or colleague. Talk about ways to overcome them and recognize there's a lot you can do. Read the list above to identify your concerns, and try out a few of the tips.

Pause and breathe. It's amazing what a time-out can do. Whether it's right before a speech or in the middle when things aren't going so well, take five seconds to pause and breathe. If you are able, physically close your mouth—so a filler doesn't escape in the interim—and breathe in and out through your nose. You center yourself and also give your audience time to catch up to you.

LEARNING HOW TO BREATHE

When people ask me about the most important thing to learn in public speaking, I answer in one word: breathing. Yes, I know breathing sounds obvious. But breathing is an incredibly powerful tool that you never learn unless you're a performer, actor, speaker, or yoga practitioner. As a singer, breathing can make or break your career.

I'm not talking about the subconscious breathing we do instinctively; I'm talking about breathing with a specific purpose in mind. The common term you hear is diaphragmatic breathing.

This kind of purposeful breathing has two invaluable benefits in public speaking. First, it calms you down. Below, I'll show you how breathing reduces your anxiety and centers you before and during your speech. Second, it gives your voice richness and fullness, letting you command a room. Two pretty important benefits, right? Let's learn how to do it.

There are hundreds of breathing techniques; here are the ones that work for me and my clients. You'll want to stand up for this exercise. If you are unable to stand for any reason, feel free to do this while sitting tall. If you feel dizzy or light-headed during this exercise, relax and breathe normally.[4]

Get Rid of Nervous Energy

Before we focus on breathing, let's get rid of nervous energy. You can train for speaking like you train for a sport. Stand up and slowly roll your shoulders back. Shake out your hands and feet, one at a time. Slowly stretch your face wide, then scrunch it up: feel like you're chewing on air to warm up your cheeks. Exhale loudly through your mouth like you were a horse, trilling your lips. Do this unvocalized, and then with a light vocalization. You'll see an example of these exercises at www.speakwithimpactbook.com. ⊕

Breathing Part 1: Find the Right Posture

Stand tall with your feet firmly planted, shoulder-width apart. Gently breathe in through your nose while raising your arms up over your head. Then exhale through your nose while you slowly lower your arms and keep your rib cage where it is. Continue breathing through your nose. You're standing tall on both feet, and your shoulders are relaxed and back, not up by your ears. This is the right posture for speaking with confidence.

Breathing Part 2: Breathe In

Place one hand over your chest and one over your belly button. Gently take a breath in and then exhale. Which hand moves when you breathe in? It might be the hand on your chest, it might be the hand on your belly, or it might be both. I'd like you to focus on your belly when you take in a breath. Relax your chest so it doesn't heave up and down.

Put both hands over your belly button. Imagine there is a balloon inside your stomach, and as you breathe in, the balloon expands, filling with air. Your stomach gets bigger as you breathe in; then as you exhale, your stomach comes back in. This might feel like the exact *opposite* of what you normally do, but try it a few times until it feels natural; then take a break and breathe normally. Remember to keep your upper body relaxed; you shouldn't feel any discomfort using this technique.

Breathing Part 3: Speak "on the Breath"

Now that you've learned how to breathe in, let's learn how to speak while breathing out. Breathe in silently on a count of three (don't forget to use the above method), then exhale and count to four out loud, letting your breath support the words like a cushion of air. You can hear me demonstrate what this sounds like at www.speakwithimpactbook.com. ⊕ Imagine you are placing the sound in the front of your face, as if you have speakers on your cheekbones, instead of feeling the words catch in your throat.

Now relax and breathe normally. It's important to give yourself frequent breaks during these exercises. When you're ready, breathe in and exhale while saying, "Good morning!" Another breath in. As you exhale, say, "My name is [your name]." This lets you practice breathing in between sentences.

I once had nodules on my vocal cords, a terrifying experience that left me unable to sing. I visited an otolaryngologist (ear, nose, and throat doctor) at the Boston Medical Center and, on his recommendation, a speech pathologist specializing in care of the professional voice, named Hadas Golan. She emphasized the importance of breathing in and out through my nose, which acts as a filter and humidifies the air going into my throat and lungs. She also helped me become more intentional about breathing. It wasn't about taking bigger breaths; it was about pacing myself and breathing more gently. She also worked with me on articulating and placing my words more forward in my face, as I've described above. Through several months of breathing and speaking techniques with Hadas, the nodes disappeared and I didn't require surgery. To this day, I use her exercises before I speak or sing.

Frequently Asked Questions About Breathing

How can I practice this? Spend a few minutes in the morning practicing these breathing techniques. At night, practice before you go to bed. Inhaling on a count of four and exhaling (silently) on a count of five is a great way to relax and fall asleep. Other places to practice discreetly include: on airplanes, during your commute (as long as you're not driving), or during meetings or conference calls.

How long does it take before I can do this comfortably? It depends. If you've studied breathing techniques in the past, you'll be able to pick this up quickly. If you've never focused on breathing before, it may take you a little longer. Be patient with yourself and practice for a few minutes each day.

How often should I breathe like this? You don't have to use these techniques during every minute of every day. You can use them right before a speech, to calm your nerves and center yourself, and right before you introduce yourself in public. Once you're comfortable using these techniques, use them at each punctuation mark in the speech. Don't use them in front of an audience until you can do it effortlessly (and without physically touching your belly).

What if I can't hear the difference? Sometimes it takes people a little longer to pick up these techniques. Sometimes people have vocal conditions that make it difficult to hear the difference. If you have nodules on your vocal cords, or if you are a smoker, or if you have a cold, these factors prevent your voice from resonating at its fullest. If you have any questions or concerns about your voice, consider visiting an otolaryngologist and/or a speech therapist.

Practice these techniques a few times, then relax and breathe normally:

Step 1: Find the right posture (stand tall).

Step 2: Breathe in (using your belly).

Step 3: Exhale and say, "Good morning" (on the breath).

Enlist a practice partner and try a "before/after" exercise. Breathe normally and introduce yourself. Then breathe using these techniques and introduce yourself while speaking "on the breath." Your partner will probably hear the difference, but you might not. Try doing the same thing with a memo recorder so you can hear the difference. Practice a few minutes at a time each day.

BUILDING YOUR CONFIDENCE

In my experience, confidence is one of the most important components of public speaking. If you are confident, the audience will forgive a few filler words or mistakes. If you are confident in your subject and in yourself, your audience is more likely to have confidence in *you*. This is not the same as arrogance or bluster. It's not about showing the audience that you are better than they are; it's about a deep conviction in your own value and your ability to deliver.

How do you find and build confidence? In *The Confidence Code*, Katty Kay and Claire Shipman interview experts who say that genes account for anywhere from 25 to 50 percent of our confidence.[5] Still, there is so much we can do to build it. When my team and I discuss this subject during workshops, we divide it into two areas: what *builds* confidence, and what *demonstrates* confidence.

What builds confidence? Take a minute and think about that question.

You feel more confident when:

- Someone validates your work. That's why, in our workshops, we always emphasize what people do well before we talk about what to improve. It's also important to realize that people in the audience *want* you to do well.

- You've experienced success in the past. That's why the more *successful* speeches you give, the better you feel.

- You know your subject and have the right skills. That's why public speaking training is so important.

- You have practiced and prepared. That's why speaking off the cuff is so nerve-racking.

- You feel a sense of purpose around why you do what you do. This is the answer to *Why you?*

- You value yourself and what you bring to the speech.

Conduct a self-assessment. Which of the above areas do you need to focus on to build your confidence? Notice that some of these areas depend on other people, not on you. How can you play a confidence-building role for others in your life?

Now let's look at what *demonstrates* confidence. Picture a truly confident speaker in your organization or in your community. Maybe it's a CEO or a political leader. What makes him or her *appear* confident?

- When meeting someone, it's their firm handshake and direct eye contact. If they're speaking in public, it's the meaningful hand gestures they use, a tall but relaxed posture, and eye contact with the audience.

- You can hear confidence in someone's voice. Instead of shaking and inaudible, a confident voice is clear and calm. It doesn't have to be loud, but it's strong and well supported.

- You feel it in someone's presence. It resonates around them like an energy and touches the audience.

- People who are confident speak at a fluid pace instead of rushing too fast or pausing too often.

What do you notice in this list? Confidence comes across more in nonverbal communication than in the words themselves. It's an energy that affects the words. But the right words (authentic language) will affect that energy.

Focus first on what *builds* confidence, then focus on what *demonstrates* confidence. Essentially, you have to build your confidence in order to show it.

The Core Value Statement. One of the most powerful confidence-building tools we use is the Core Value Statement. I developed this tool after reading a research report from the University of California showing that individuals who affirmed their personal values before a speech experienced less stress when giving that speech.[6] Here's how it goes:

1. Make a list of your core values.

2. Circle one that resonates the most.

3. Write a paragraph about *how you live that value every day*.

Here's an example that came from Global Public Speaking's business manager, Meghan Gonzalez.

Integrity is a core value of my work and is the basis for all of my professional and personal interactions. I live this value every day by being honest with my friends, family, and coworkers, and holding myself accountable for all that I do. Integrity always takes precedence over easy choices. I strive to be a role model for my team and my family, while exhibiting the strong moral characteristics that I look for in others.

Give it a try. How do you live your values every day? The end result is your Core Value Statement. Visit www.speakwithimpactbook.com for a handout that guides you through this exercise. ⊕ Keep it nearby and read it *out loud* before every speech, presentation, or difficult conversation. It grounds you in who you are and what's important to you, which is an incredible confidence-builder.

Breathe in and out. Find a quiet place and sit tall in a comfortable chair. Close your eyes and focus solely on your breathing. Feel your stomach gently expand as you breathe in and relax as you breathe out. Breathe in slowly and silently on a count of 3 and exhale slowly on a count of 4. If you're pressed for time, even one minute of this breathing will help you calm down.

Mental Rehearsal. Go back to the mental rehearsal exercise we discussed in Chapter 5 and use it to calm yourself, center yourself, and build confidence that you will do an outstanding job. Imagine yourself giving a powerful speech that has a meaningful impact on your audience, and you'll feel like you are already a successful speaker.

CHAPTER 8

Give the Speech

All Those Last-Minute Details

GETTING READY

The day of the speech or presentation is approaching. You've worked through this book and feel comfortable with the messaging, you feel like the language is authentic and impactful, you've practiced your delivery, and you've used breathing to calm your nerves. Great job! Now your mind turns to all those other little things that make or break a speech, worrying about the "What If?" scenarios where things can go wrong. Let's walk through the final steps to giving the speech or presentation. These are the tested-and-true techniques of a road warrior who gives nearly a hundred presentations a year and has developed a routine for success. Don't make the same mistakes I've made!

DEALING WITH LOGISTICS

Practice, but not too much. On the morning of the speech, I will run through the speech or presentation out loud in its entirety, using the notes I've created. I will normally practice in front of a mirror and watch my body language at the same time. It boosts my confidence and reminds me that I'm ready.

Know exactly where the venue is. You wouldn't believe how many times I've flown into a city, only to realize I don't know the exact location of the next day's speech, *nor do I have a cell-phone number for the organizer.* A quick preparation checklist fixed that; make sure you have all the details you need in advance. You can see the pre-workshop checklist all our Global Public Speaking trainers use at www.speakwithimpactbook.com. ⊕

Get there early and prepare the room. Did previous occupants use the room late into the night and leave half-eaten sandwiches? Are all the audiovisuals locked in a cabinet and no one has the key? Get to the room at least an hour before audience members arrive and make sure everything is in order. One of my biggest stressors is having participants walk in while I'm still setting things up, which means I can't greet them personally. Have the phone number of a local contact so you can call someone for assistance. At Global Public Speaking, our goal is to be bored thirty minutes before anyone arrives at our presentations or workshops. Why? Because it means we got there early, fixed any problems, and are ready to go.

Where in the room will you be standing? Determine that in advance, and set up what you need: water, your notes, and perhaps your cell phone using a clock app that can keep you on time. Large conference rooms might display a timer to keep you on track, but in smaller rooms you'll need to use your own. Note: If you use your phone during a presentation, *put it on airplane mode.* I remember being in the middle of a presentation when I received a call from a friend who was deathly ill in the hospital. The phone was on silent, but the caller ID sent my mind racing and distracted me from the presentation.

Will someone introduce you? If so, bring a printed introduction for that person. When writing that intro, read it out loud as you'd want the introducer to read it and make sure it is written for the ear. Email it to the organizer in advance, but bring a hard copy printed in a large font.

Greet people as they arrive. Many times, clients will confide in me that they hate speaking to a group of strangers, so I recommend greeting people as they walk in. A big smile and a firm handshake help you connect on a personal level. Ask them what they hope to get from your presentation or how familiar they are with the subject. When you are curious about others, it distracts you from how nervous you are about your speech. Remember that this is an opportunity to build a relationship between you and each member of the audience. You can start that relationship the moment someone enters the room and continue it long after the speech ends.

WHAT TO WEAR

While we might not like to admit it, people judge us based partly on our attire. Along with our body language, our attire communicates when we walk into a room, before we even open our mouths to speak. Should you wear a business suit or T-shirt and jeans? Think back to the first two questions you ask yourself in public speaking: *Who is your audience? What is your goal?* The culture of the audience in part determines what you will wear. It's important to find a balance between what's comfortable to you and what's appropriate for the situation. If you come from a different culture and want to wear something that represents that culture, do so proudly. Be purposeful about it, recognizing that your clothing sends *a* message but shouldn't be *the* message of your speech.

A friend of mine was running for office in a rural region of the country. In the coming weeks, he was going to address workers at a local factory.

"What are you going to wear?" I asked him.

"I'll tell you what I'm *not* going to wear: the three-piece suit I'm wearing right now," he responded. "I'll wear more casual clothes so they see me as more approachable." It's not about being disingenuous;

it's about choosing attire that communicates the message you want to send.

If you're a young professional dressing for your first big corporate interview, you're not going to wear sandals and shorts to your interview. You'll wear a business suit that communicates professionalism. But if you're a software engineer interviewing at a startup and you show up in a business suit, you might be communicating conformity or a lack of creativity—the opposite of what you want to demonstrate.

Here are some general guidelines I'd like you to keep in mind regarding attire:

- *Be comfortable.* I've had female clients ask me if they need to wear high heels in a formal business setting, even if they feel uncomfortable in heels. My answer: no. Simply make sure that your flats look professional instead of old and scuffed. Those same clients have also asked about whether they can wear their long hair down or if they should keep it back. For both men and women, the answer is the same: make sure your hair doesn't hide your face or fall into your eyes. Do you sweat when you are nervous? Wear dark colors so the audience won't notice sweat stains when you move your arms. Dress in layers, so you can remove your jacket and still be comfortable. I give this advice to women going through menopause so that they can make themselves more comfortable if they have a hot flash onstage. On the day of your speech, you will be nervous about many things: the message, the audience, etc. You don't want to feel uncomfortable about your clothing.

- *Match your attire to your goal.* What image are you hoping to present to the audience? Do you want to project confidence, style, or power? Do you want to come across as down-to-earth and quirky? Choose your clothes according to your goal.

- *Think of the venue.* If you are speaking on a panel, you'll most likely be seated on a chair on a raised podium, with people's eye level falling somewhere below your waist. If you're wearing pants, make sure they are comfortable to sit in. If you're wearing a skirt or dress, make sure the hemline is long enough so that your audience can't look up your skirt.

- **When in doubt, ask someone.** Ask a colleague who has spoken at a similar event, or ask the organizer about the dress code. Personally, I like to err on the safe side, which harkens back to my mother's advice when I was in middle school: *Allison,* you *set the dress code.*

TAKE CARE OF YOUR BODY

Speaking in public is like playing a sport. It is a physical and mental activity that requires training and preparation. Here are some tips for keeping your body in shape and ready to speak.

- **Get enough sleep** the night before the speech or presentation. Personally, I need seven to eight hours of sleep before a speech. I can speak with six hours of sleep, but I'm not at my best and I can't do it repeatedly. Protect your time and get enough rest. You might be staying at a hotel the night before the speech, so recognize what you need to sleep at a hotel. For me, it's a white-noise app on my smartphone and noise-cancelling headphones.

- **Get some sort of exercise.** Your body is a physical instrument that responds to physical stimulus. Go for a brisk walk, get to the gym, or do some sort of workout in your room the day of the speech—for me, it's push-ups, sit-ups, running in place, and stretching.

- *Meditate.* I find that spending time in meditation the day of the speech (and every day) helps me calm down. I sit in a chair for fifteen minutes and focus on my breathing, using the techniques I've taught you in Chapter 7. There are numerous methods of meditation; use what works for you.

- *Drink lots of water.* Water hydrates your vocal cords, so drink water leading up to the speech and feel free to have a bottle or glass nearby on the lectern or table.

- *Protect your voice.* If you have a cold on the day of your speech, use cough drops to soothe your throat and stick to herbal tea with honey instead of caffeinated beverages. If you've lost your voice, try gargling with warm saltwater to get it back. And try vocal rest—no talking at all—in the twenty-four hours leading up to your speech.

What to Avoid Before You Speak

As an opera singer, I learned early on what to avoid before going on-stage. Certain foods and beverages would reduce the quality of my singing voice. They have the same effect when speaking.

- *Avoid loud venues.* Networking at the bar the night before your speech might be fun, but it fatigues your voice when you have to yell to be heard. Try to network in quieter spaces with fewer people, or get there early and leave early.

- *Avoid alcohol.* Singing karaoke taught me that while drinking alcohol might improve how I sounded to *myself*, it did not improve how I sounded to my *audience*. In a speech or presentation, you're putting yourself in a dangerous position by going onstage in a diminished mental capacity. If you're nervous, use the natural methods I've talked about in this book instead of relying on alcohol.

- **Reduce caffeine.** Notice I didn't say "avoid caffeine," because I can't do that myself. Recognize that caffeine dries out your vocal cords (as does alcohol), so drink herbal tea with honey right before you speak.

MY PRE-SPEECH RITUAL

I remember coaching a group of college students ten years ago, on the day they presented their leadership projects to donors, parents, and professors. They clustered around me in the hallway outside the conference room, clamoring for help to calm down. They were so nervous, they couldn't eat dinner. We went through the following exercise, which I now use with each and every client, from young professionals to senior executives. It only takes five minutes, but it completely changes your mind-set about speaking. You can watch a video guiding you through this exercise at www.speakwithimpactbook.com. ⊕ Whether you use mine or develop a new one, find a pre-speech ritual that works for you.

Step 1: Find a quiet place where you can be alone. It might be your office, your hotel room, or even a public restroom at the venue where you are speaking.

Step 2: Get rid of nervous energy. Start by shaking out your arms and legs, one at a time. Stretch out your face to lightly loosen your jaw. Do vocalized lip trills to warm up your voice. Find the right posture for speaking: raise your arms up while you take a gentle breath in, then slowly exhale while you lower your arms, keeping your rib cage where it is. See Chapter 7 for more breathing tips.

Step 3: Center yourself. Take gentle breaths in through your nose, feeling the energy fill your body. As you exhale, center yourself and be present in the moment. Don't think about anything other than your breath. Take a breath in on a count of three and slowly exhale on a count of four.

Step 4: Remind yourself, *Why you?* Answer that question *out loud*. Read your Core Value Statement (from Chapter 7) out loud. This exercise prevents your mind from going blank because it connects you with your sense of purpose; you stop focusing on your nerves and instead focus on your message and its impact on your audience.

Step 5: Run through your opening and closing. The only parts I recommend you memorize in your speech are the opening and closing so that when you walk out onstage, you are prepared to start and end with power and purpose.

It takes five minutes to go through this exercise, but it can change your entire outlook on your upcoming speech. Give it a try!

DEALING WITH BEING ONSTAGE

You've warmed up, centered yourself, and prepared a great speech or presentation. You've walked out onstage or to the front of the conference room and are looking at a sea of expectant faces all turned toward you. Hopefully, some of them are smiling. Hopefully, not too many are on their digital devices. What now?

Don't overthink things. Don't feel like you need to ease into it with a *So, yeah* intro. *Pause and breathe*, smile, turn to one person, and say your opening sentence. Then look at someone else and say the next sentence. Suddenly, you're thinking about the message instead of about your nerves. The audience is smiling and nodding, a few people are taking notes, and you're getting the hang of it. As you speak, your sense of purpose increases and you focus on the power of your message. You make eye contact to ensure that everyone is with you, and you use body language to reinforce your words. Your voice is strong and purposeful. Your words have impact. You're doing this!

There will be things that go wrong. There is no perfect speech, ever—but it's not about what goes wrong with your speech, it's about your confidence in handling those situations.

What if your mind goes blank while you are speaking? That's why you have your bullet points in front of you with the main messages. Simply *pause and breathe*, nod thoughtfully, glance down at your notes, and move on to your next point.

What if the AV doesn't work? Even if you've arrived early and triple-checked the AV, something can still go wrong. You have a few options here: you can keep calm and try to fix it yourself, you can take a quick break, or you can continue without using AV by saying, *Let's keep going and we'll come back to this.*

What if your audience seems distracted? You can ask the audience questions or have them answer a question in groups of two to reinvigorate their attention. Refer to the sidebar about reading the room.

What if I pass out from nerves? You won't. *Pause and breathe* to calm yourself down and focus on your message.

READING THE ROOM

Communication is a two-way street: while you're giving the speech, the audience is responding in different ways. Here are some positive and negative signs to look for. Keep in mind that audience reactions vary widely depending on culture, so take the time to understand the culture(s) of your audience in advance.

Positive Reactions

When the audience reacts positively to your speech, you can feel it. There's an energy or electricity in the room; sometimes you'll even forget about time. Here are some signs:

- Making eye contact
- Nodding heads
- Laughing/smiling in the right places
- Asking questions/making comments
- Taking notes

Usually, these positive reactions happen when you've taken the time to frame your message in a way that is relevant and urgent for your audience. They also happen when you care about your message and deliver it with energy, conviction, and confidence.

Negative Reactions

I always caution people not to get carried away when the audience seems disengaged. Sometimes it could be because of your presentation. Sometimes it's due to outside circumstances. Here are some signs:

- Looking at their phone or digital device
- Defensive body language (arms crossed, frowning expression)
- Head resting in their hands
- Not making eye contact with you
- Falling asleep

When do these negative reactions happen? Sometimes your speech or presentation is at the end of a long day. Sometimes the audience has heard endless lectures with no audience engagement. Maybe the room is cold. It also happens when you don't take the time to present material in a way that's relevant to them, or you yourself are bored.

When I see the above reactions from a number of people during my speech (not just one person), I will include one of the following techniques:

- **Open it up for questions.** "Let me stop here for a moment. What questions do you have?"
- **Ask the audience a question.** "Who else has dealt with this topic? What did you learn?"
- **Groups of two.** Ask the audience to pair up and talk through the pros and cons of something you've discussed in the speech.
- **Summarize your main points.** Summarize what you've said so far, to make sure the audience is with you.
- **Tell a story.** Insert a relevant story that lets the audience sit back and listen.
- **Table discussion.** Throw out a challenge and have people discuss the solution at their tables, then report back by table.

> If you know the context of your speech in advance—room setup, the timing in the day, the composition of the audience—then you can pre-plan those energizers throughout the speech.
>
> Use the above indicators to read the room while you are speaking, and be flexible enough to change your outline in response to your audience's reaction. The result will be a more engaging speech and a more engaged audience.

FOLLOWING THE SPEECH

Congratulations! You've given the speech or presentation! You can go home and collapse now, right? Wrong. You can give the same speech a hundred times and never improve. How you debrief the speech is a critical part of your development as a speaker. Within ten minutes of concluding your speech or presentation, debrief the experience by asking yourself these three questions.

1. **What went well?** Be specific.

2. **What didn't go well?** Be honest.

3. **What are you going to do differently next time?** Be strategic.

I've created a Speaker's Logbook so our clients can keep track of their feedback from one speech or presentation to the next. You can find one at www.speakwithimpactbook.com. ⊕ We also have speech feedback forms you can download and give to a friend or colleague in the audience before you speak. Make time to speak with that person immediately following the speech so you can receive valuable feedback while it's fresh. Add that feedback to your Logbook.

If there was a video of your speech, *watch the video*. I hate doing it, too, but I learn from it every time, and it's a critical part of my leadership communication workshops. You notice things like your voice trailing off at the end of a sentence or your energy not being big enough for the room. Athletes watch playbacks of their performance, and musicians do the same. If you're serious about making progress, you must see how you're actually doing, as opposed to relying on how you felt. Enlist a friend or colleague to give you feedback as well. Oftentimes, they will have observations that you can't (or won't) see.

When you watch the video of your speech, you may be pleasantly surprised with how it went! In that case, how about sharing it on social media or posting it online, if your organization will allow it? If you're interested in more speaking opportunities, then posting a quality video online is a great way to broadcast your speaking skills to interested meeting planners.

Based on your self-assessment of how the speech went and the feedback you receive from others and from the video, it's time to make a plan to continue making progress. Should you join Toastmasters where you can practice your skills in a safe environment? Will you take a formal course at a local college? Will you look for online programs where you can brush up on your skills? Will you find a practice buddy to help you through the process? Or will you get an executive coach to help you? All of these are valid options.

Public speaking is a skill; if you give one speech and never speak again, you won't develop the skill. Hopefully, you have a renewed sense of purpose and passion for speaking that will push you to find new opportunities to speak, both at work and elsewhere. Many times, going through communication training at work will provide skills that you can use in your community as well, when you have to confront a neighborhood development project or speak up for a special program in your child's school. There are opportunities all around you to use your voice to make an impact.

This first half of the book provided a step-by-step approach to writing, practicing, and delivering a speech or presentation. In the second half, we'll look at specific speaking situations—from presenting with slides, to speaking off the cuff, to moderating a panel. Use this second half as a reference manual; find the sections that apply to the kind of speaking situations you face so that you can command the room and influence others on any occasion.

CHAPTER 9

Illustrate the Speech

How to Use Visual Aids and Technology

UNDERSTANDING THE ROLE OF VISUAL AIDS

I don't use many visual aids when speaking. My goal is to teach people how to connect on a personal level with an audience, and I find that props too often become a barrier. To quote Tamara Elliott Rogers, who served as Harvard University's Vice President for Alumni Affairs and Development for over a decade, "I like to power my own points!"

Having said that, there are ways you can use visual aids to effectively reinforce your message. Here are some ways:

- *Capture your audience's attention.* Used effectively, a visual aid can capture (or regain) your audience's attention by showing something unique and unexpected. If their minds have been wandering, then a physical prop or unusual slide will bring their attention back by saying, "Listen up, something new and interesting is happening." It's an effective way to break up the monotony of a presentation.

- *Paint a picture for your audience*. Presentation slides let you go beyond words to paint a picture in your audience's mind. Why spend five minutes describing a scenario when you can instantly show a picture?

- *Take your audience on an emotional journey.* A brief, inspirational film clip can tug at your audience's heartstrings and create empathy with your subject. If you lead a nonprofit, you can show a clip of your work in the field.

- *Reinforce a point.* You can reinforce an important point through a slide or image. If one of your points is that turnover at your company has reached unprecedented levels, show a graph that compares the trend to previous years and creates a sense of urgency.

- *Address different ways of learning.* We learn through both listening and reading, so provide both options to maximize learning. If your audience members have different levels of language fluency, it can be helpful to hear and see the message simultaneously.

- *Converse with your audience.* With technology, props can make a presentation much more interactive. You can use digital tools to poll your audience, solicit and answer questions, send handouts, and enable social media.

- *Remember your notes or read your script.* In larger conference rooms, you will find monitors at the foot of the stage, turned toward the presenter, that display the time remaining or bullet points of your notes. You can use a teleprompter to display your script.

- *Broaden your audience.* You can use streaming technology to broadcast your message around the world. Companies will use this for remote workers participating in training. Or you can use Facebook Live to broadcast your message online for a much wider audience.

Let's look at the types of visual aids available to see what's the best fit. Regardless of which ones you choose, make sure you understand the room, the venue's capabilities, and the size of your audience.

USING PHYSICAL AIDS

The beauty of using physical aids is that they work without electricity. Prepare them in advance, and you can rely on them without worrying about Internet access or having the right adapters. Just remember to bring them with you or ship them to the venue in advance.

Props. In the movie *Up in the Air,* George Clooney sets a backpack onstage and uses it as a metaphor throughout the speech.[1] It's a powerful scene that demonstrates both the use of props and visualization. A physical prop can be a great way to surprise your audience (the "unexpected" principle of stickiness, from Chip Heath and Dan Heath). It allows you to be creative with something simple. If you're giving a speech on the benefits of home ownership, you can walk onstage, take out a pen, and say, "Twenty years ago, I used this pen to close on my very first home. It was one of the proudest moments of my life."

Swag or gifts for the audience. Author and keynote speaker Bruce Turkel gives harmonicas to his audiences to show the power of creativity and a customer-centric focus, and I've watched musician and keynote speaker Mike Rayburn give away an actual guitar to an unsuspecting audience member. These unexpected gifts both engage the audience and reinforce the speaker's main messages. You don't have to be a professional speaker—and you don't have to give away a musical instrument—to use this type of prop. A small but unexpected treat can be a great way to engage your audience.

Handouts or pitch book. If your presentation is informative and your audience will be discussing it with others after you speak, consider bringing handouts or a pitch book. They could summarize your main points and include all the graphs and data you don't want to project onto the screen. I normally give out these materials at the *end* of my presentation so people stay focused. However, when presenting from a pitch book, you may have to walk through the book with your audience. In that case, my colleague and public speaking expert Trudi Bresner recommends that you keep the audience focused on you by using key points, stories, and anecdotes that aren't in the pitch book.

Flip chart or whiteboard. Despite all the advances in technology, sometimes you just want to pick up a marker and write. I like to solicit audience members' questions and challenges about public speaking and write them down on a flip chart at the front of the room, then refer to those questions throughout my workshop. This makes the presentation more of an interactive brainstorming session than a one-way lecture.

USING TECHNOLOGY IN YOUR SPEECH

Let's look at some current ways to use technology in your speech, recognizing that there are always new and exciting tools on the horizon. Throughout this section, I will use the term "device," which can refer to your smartphone, tablet, or any other gadget invented between now and the time you read this book. No matter which technology you use, if it relies on an Internet connection, make sure the room has the right connection to support the technology.

Show a film clip. You can show a short film clip to introduce a speech or to break up a longer topic. I've seen conferences use film clips to distract the audience while organizers set the stage for a panel discussion. If you work in international development and want to demonstrate the impact of your work in the field, you can show a brief film clip of volunteers at work or the human effects of the project. Make sure you have permission to show whichever clip you use.

Use devices for practice and feedback. New apps listen to your practice speech and record how many filler words you use. The one that shows the most promise is Ummo, which actually chimes in real time when you say a filler (note: only use this when practicing).[2] You can also record yourself on your phone and play it back or send it to a friend, colleague, or coach for feedback. You could use videoconferencing to practice your speech with others. I routinely use videoconferencing for coaching clients on the other side of the world.

Use devices for audience engagement. You can poll your audience and project their responses onto a screen. You can ask the audience to tweet questions and you can either answer them onstage or after the event. You can ask audiences to text a certain number to sign up for a mailing list or download your slides. When I use polling during a workshop, I'll normally start with a word cloud: I ask the audience to take out their phones, open the app that they downloaded for that conference, and type one word about how they feel about public speaking. The answers show up in real time on a screen in front of the audience. Responses will usually include: nervous, anxious, and fearful. After the workshop, I'll do another word cloud and ask, "*Now* how do you feel about public speaking?" Hopefully, responses will include: confident, excited, and ready.

In some conferences, organizers will set up a large screen on one side of the room to show real-time social media engagement with the conference. That creates a secondary discussion and allows people to connect online, hopefully leading to more in-person connections. You can also use streaming technology like Facebook Live to broadcast content to a virtual audience.

Use devices to control your slides. As a speaker, you can use a device to control your slides or display your notes. There are new gadgets that let you control your slides with arm muscles.[3] I recommend using these tools only if you can use them comfortably—never try them out in front of an audience before practicing extensively.

Use a monitor to show your notes. In a large room, I've seen speakers use a monitor at their feet to display their notes. This works if it's just notes; but if you read from a script, then you'll be looking down the entire time.

Use a teleprompter. It takes practice to read comfortably from a teleprompter. The advantage is that you can have the exact script, hopefully written in language that is natural and conversational to you, and can generally look at the audience. The downside is that it's difficult to go off script without losing your place.

I'm sure you've noticed that there was one type of visual aid I didn't mention. I'm going to devote an entire section of this chapter to presentation slides.

USING SLIDES FOR GOOD AND NOT FOR EVIL

Presentation slides can show a gripping picture, reinforce a key message, illustrate a surprising trend, or show an emotional video. There are some excellent books on slide design by presentation experts, such as *slide-ology: The Art and Science of Creating Great Presentations* by Nancy Duarte[4] and *Presentation Zen: Simple Ideas on Presentation Design and Delivery* by Garr Reynolds.[5] ⊕ For our purposes, I'll go over some of the common misuses of slides and show you how to use them effectively.

Common Misuses of Slides

Misuse #1: To remind you what to say. When people don't have time to prepare, they throw their written notes into a slide to jog their memory. I still remember one of my earliest speech-writing clients. I was designing a presentation for an executive in Boston. I specifically remember one slide he asked me to create, consisting of a few random words that didn't make any sense. I asked him what they were supposed to signify. He responded, "Don't worry, it just reminds me what to say next." Whenever you're using slides, design them with your audience in mind.

Misuse #2: To cover a lot of information in a short period of time. Remember that the more you say, the less people will hear. If you throw endless charts and graphs up on the screen, they will distract your audience. Clicking through slides while saying, "We don't have time to cover this, but I wanted to put it up," confuses your audience and dilutes your main messages. If you want to convey extra information, create handouts.

Misuse #3: To deflect attention from yourself. Some speakers will put all their content onto the slides so that the audience looks at the slides instead of at the speaker. This is a missed opportunity to connect with your audience and leads to the presentation feeling more like a lecture than a conversation. Use the techniques in this book to build your confidence so that you are comfortable connecting with the audience.

Many companies not only dictate the use of slides, they dictate the use of *bad slides* with too much text and too many graphs. You don't always have a choice when using slides, though the more senior you become in an organization, the more you have the power to change those expectations.

How to Use Slides Effectively

Before designing your slides, first figure out the content. Then ask how slides can effectively reinforce that content. Make a list of your key points and then ask yourself:

- What images could illustrate these points?

- What charts or graphs could reinforce these numbers?

- What quotes can I put on the screen?

- What technology software do I want to use?

Unfortunately, it takes longer to design good slides than it does to design bad slides, though new technologies are making this more approachable and you can usually outsource the design. Regardless, it still takes a lot of time to distill your content and think about the most creative, concise ways to present information visually.

If someone else designs your slides, make sure you share your outline and message with that person *in advance* so that the slides reinforce what you'd like to say. It's hard to merge your message with someone else's slides after the fact.

Here are some of the most important things to keep in mind when designing slides.

Phrases, not sentences. When you put full sentences on a slide, you have a tendency to turn your back to the audience and read the text word for word. In addition, the audience can read faster than you can speak, so they read the slides instead of listening to you. This is a missed opportunity to connect with the audience. Put phrases on your slides instead of full sentences.

I remember the first day of class in college. I was thinking about taking one particular course taught by a global expert. I arrived to class eager to learn from this professor. He welcomed everyone, turned to the front of the room, and proceeded to read his slides, word for word, for the entire lecture. The slides themselves looked like they had been copied and pasted from his teaching notes. As the lecture wore on, I got a sinking feeling in the pit of my stomach. How could I listen to this person for an entire semester? I could hardly listen for one hour!

Large font size. Guy Kawasaki, author of *The Art of the Start 2.0,* recommends you take the age of the oldest person in your audience, divide it in half, and use that number as the *minimum* font size in your presentation.[6] As a general rule, use a font size that can be comfortably read by someone older than you sitting in the back of the room. That includes using a sans-serif font that's easily readable on a screen. I highly recommend picking up a copy of Guy's book and reading the chapter, "The Art of Pitching."

One of my biggest pet peeves is when a speaker says, "I know this font size is tiny, but bear with me." *No, I will not bear with you. You're giving me a headache, so I need to look away. As a result, you've lost my attention, unless you're my boss, in which case I have to pay attention but I'm not happy about it.* Is this what you want going through the minds of your audience members?

One image, one sentence per slide. I'm a big fan of Steve Jobs's presentation design: one image, one phrase per slide. Think back to the iPhone launch in 2007: black background, one quote, one number, and one image per slide. [7]⊕

Bad slide design can actually be dangerous when it hides critical information. There is a crushing example from the 2003

Columbia space shuttle explosion, where key points were buried within complex slides, causing NASA to underestimate the risk involved in returning the shuttle safely back to Earth.[8] When you present a critical piece of information, put it front and center and give it its own slide. Lives can depend on it.

Logistics When Using Slides

Know your technology. Spend lots of time becoming comfortable with your fancy new presentation gadget or software before you use it in front of your audience. Otherwise, you'll be troubleshooting in public and lose your credibility.

Run through your material with slides in advance. Speaking with slides always takes longer than speaking without slides, because looking at the slides has a tendency to make you say more than you intended. Practice and time the speech with the slides to make sure you keep to your limit.

Proofread your slides. Inconsistent fonts, extra spaces between words, and misspelled words are errors that can instantly make you look lazy and unprepared. Proofread your slides with a critical eye, or have someone else proof them who hasn't been staring at them for two hours. Your slides are an extension of your professionalism and brand.

Arrange for AV assistance in advance. If you're using slides, make sure the event organizers have the right equipment in the room. Ask yourself what extra equipment you might need, like adapters or cables. I'm a Mac user, so I always carry my own set of adapters to connect to the projector. Email your slides to the organizers in advance and bring the slides on a flash drive as a backup. Get to the room an hour before people arrive so you can set up the slides and make sure they work.

The most important tip for using slides is this:

Always be prepared to present without slides. Despite all your best efforts, the AV might not work, your computer might not connect, or no one can find the password for the computer on the lectern. When this happens, and it will happen at some point, do *not* follow the example of one speaker I heard a few years ago. I was attending an event in Arlington, Virginia, for government contractors. Unfortunately, one of the speakers couldn't get his laptop to work with the projector. So the speaker proceeded to describe every one of his slides to the audience out loud, *including the cartoons.* Instead of speaking for ten minutes, he talked for over forty-five minutes. But he had lost his audience in the first two minutes.

You can use slides effectively, but remember that it takes time, creativity, and a focus on the experience of your audience. Giving a speech or presentation is about connecting with your audience and moving them to take action. Look at technology as a way to *enhance* that connection.

Look through your upcoming speech or presentation and determine which props will be most effective, *if any.* If you always use slides, ask yourself if they are necessary and if they will add impact to your presentation. Give yourself plenty of time to prepare your props and practice with them before the speech.

INTERVIEW WITH SIDD CHOPRA

For a look into the future, I interviewed my friend and colleague Sidd Chopra. Sidd is an entrepreneur, systems developer, author, and award-winning speaker whose organization LookWiser.com is constantly inventing new public speaking tools. In fact, I met him at a National Speakers Association conference where he was testing out a new device that allows speakers to control their slides and multiple tablet-based prompters wirelessly with one presentation controller. Given Sidd's interest in the intersection of technology and presentations, I spoke with him about the future use of technology in presentations.

He said, "We have two different, often opposing objectives: First, our need to connect with one another on a human level. Second, our need to work faster, cheaper, and further than ever. Videoconferencing is effective but doesn't replace the need to communicate in person. A smile, the warmth of a handshake, can't easily be reproduced in a remote environment. If we're not careful, communication can actually create a *false narrative about someone.* If the speaker doesn't use digital tools effectively, that person could come across as disengaged or cold. He or she could sound curt or sarcastic when trying to be friendly or funny."

Having said that, Sidd then turned to technical tools we might use in the future. "I can see using augmented reality for speaker's notes and virtual reality creating different audience experiences. What's really exciting is the potential use of holograms. Medical schools are experimenting with digital cadavers to let students practice before they work on real cadavers. Imagine giving a presentation about cancer and using a 3-D hologram to show the audience an actual body! You could move the hologram with your hand, remove a lung, and show your audience where the cancer is."

We also discussed the potential for speakers to use holograms as an actual medium. Tony Robbins famously gave the "longest running 'live 2-way' holographic performance ever" when he gave a speech in Melbourne, Australia—while he was located in Miami, Florida.[9] ⊕ For frequent speakers who practically live on airplanes, this leads to a number of quality-of-life benefits, though the technology costs are quite high at this point. Sidd also mentioned robotic avatars taking the place of actual people in a conference.

In a future edition of this book, we'll discuss updated technological applications in speeches. In the meantime, know that there are some exciting developments in the works that can help you engage with your audience in new ways—but remember to stay focused on human connection.

USING A MICROPHONE

How do you use a microphone when giving a speech? *Should* you use a microphone? Too often, I see people stand up at conferences and shout, "You can all hear me, right?" And when no one has the nerve to say "no," the speaker goes on to shout their speech. Or, they take the microphone and hold it down by their belly button, where it can't pick up any sound. If your audience can't hear you, you can't move them to action.

I've used microphones both for speaking and singing and know that using a microphone is an important way to fill the room with your message and get your voice heard. Here are some tips to do that effectively:

- *Always be willing to use a microphone.* In any audience, you will have varying levels of hearing and language fluency, regardless of the language you are speaking; make it easy for people to hear you. It's healthier for your voice—and more pleasant for your audience's ears—if you don't have to yell. If you are offering comments during a conference, stand up and use a mic if one is available. If there is a mic runner, wait for him or her to hand you the mic; it ensures that everyone can hear you and—as a result—increases your credibility and authority.

- *Determine in advance if you will need a microphone.* You'll want to use a mic if the audience is larger than twenty people or the event will be recorded. If you'd like to use the video for any reason at all, then use a mic for high-quality sound.

- *Decide which type of microphone to use.* At a conference, you can usually choose between a handheld and a hands-free mic. I choose a hands-free microphone, such as a lavaliere/lapel mic or an earset mic, so it doesn't disrupt my natural hand gestures. Avoid using the mic attached to the lectern, because it prevents you from walking around to engage the audience. If you *must* use the lectern mic, adjust the mic height in advance; you can also move the mic to the side of the lectern and stand on the side so it's easier for people to see you.

- *Do a sound check to test battery and volume in advance.* There might not be a sound technician available to help you; always check the battery and volume level before you walk onstage. You can say something like, "Testing, testing," or, "Check 1, check 2," instead of, "Um, is this thing on?"

- *Decide where to put a lapel mic:* If you're wearing a suit, you can clip the lapel mic to your lapel (hence the name), near the top of your button-down shirt, or on your tie about six inches from your face (the distance depends on how much sound the mic picks up); clip the transmitter on the back of your belt loop. Ladies, if you're wearing a dress without a belt loop, you could clip the receiver on the top back of your dress; it's a little uncomfortable, but you will get used to it. Wherever you put the mic, ensure that it isn't covered by hair or clothing, as that affects the sound quality. And if you know you'll be using a mic, wear clothing that you can easily attach the mic to. Note: Attach the mic *before* turning it on; when you are done, turn the mic off *before* taking it off.

- *Cough away from the mic.* It happens: sometimes we have to cough or sneeze onstage. Remember to turn *away* from the mic; otherwise the entire room will resonate with your booming sneeze.

- *Know how to hold a handheld microphone.* Ask the sound technician whether the microphone is omnidirectional (picks up sound from all sides) or directional (you have to speak directly into it) so you know how to hold the mic. As a general rule, hold the mic about two or three inches from your face, just under your mouth, at a 45-degree angle. When you move your head, move your hand with it so that your mic follows your mouth. Use your free hand to make hand gestures.

- *Speak with a strong, clear voice.* Don't try to yell, and don't assume that it's okay to whisper. The microphone amplifies the voice itself; make sure it's amplifying a strong, confident voice.

- *If the mic stops working, don't panic.* Sometimes there will be a problem with the sound. Relax and don't let it overwhelm you: *pause and breathe.* You could pick up a nearby mic, speak without the mic, or, if appropriate, take a five-minute break to address the issue. The more relaxed you are, the more relaxed the audience will be.

- *Assume the mic is always on!* Sometimes the sound technician will tell you that the mic has been turned off, but if you are wearing a mic, always assume that others can hear your conversation or activities. Act accordingly.

Rather than be intimidated by it, look at the microphone as an opportunity to amplify your message. Remind yourself *why* your speech subject is important to you and use that energy and enthusiasm to fuel your passion when speaking. The mic is there to make your job easier.

CHAPTER 10

Prepare for the Unexpected

How to Speak Off the Cuff and Answer Questions

EMBRACING IMPROMPTU SPEAKING

I know what you're thinking. *I'm fine giving a speech when I have time to prepare. But a lot of my speaking happens extemporaneously at a meeting.* Indeed, speaking off the cuff is a different kind of skill from prepared speaking. Regardless of your industry or job, all of us speak off the cuff every single day. Let's look at the difference.

A **prepared speech or presentation** is something you learn about in advance: you accept an invitation (or you don't have a choice), you are put on the agenda, and (hopefully) you spend time preparing.

An *impromptu speech or presentation* is when you are given little to no prior notice. During a meeting, your boss asks, "So, what do you recommend?" in front of your colleagues. You're on a call and the client asks you questions you didn't anticipate. You're at a rally or demonstration and are so overwhelmed with purpose that you take the mic and start speaking from the heart while the cameras are rolling.

Why is impromptu speaking so important? In many organizations, your bosses will assess your leadership readiness based in part on how you speak up during a meeting. When you don't speak up, many people will assume you have nothing to say. I realize that's a false assumption; and for those introverts who prefer not to speak in a meeting, you're fighting a battle against those assumptions.

The more senior you become in an organization, the more time you spend communicating the messages of the organization and the more your words guide the actions of others. Each time you speak, even when you are unprepared, your words carry incredible weight and power.

I remember one of my most painful impromptu presentations. I was a young public diplomacy officer at the Israeli Consulate, attending a community meeting on behalf of a diplomat who couldn't attend. I showed up ready to listen to others and take notes. But at the start of the meeting, the host turned to me and said: "Allison, we're so glad the Israeli Consulate is represented here today, and we'd love for you to start the meeting with a few remarks, especially in light of what happened this morning in Israel."

Gulp. What? Guess who didn't check the news that day? So I did what anyone in politics would have done; I bridged. I said, "What happened this morning in Israel only further reinforces what the foreign minister said last week." To this day, I look back at that experience and cringe. It reinforces the importance of preparation before every meeting.

Why is impromptu speaking so hard? One of the biggest causes of public speaking jitters is not having enough time to prepare. Impromptu speaking is, by definition, speaking without any preparation. Of course you will be nervous! In addition, people don't necessarily have a framework for handling impromptu speaking, so they simply say whatever is on their mind, for better or worse. The good news is, there are frameworks for speaking off the cuff and you can practice being in those situations. I'll show you how—and this kind of practice is going to help you every single day.

How to Approach Impromptu Speaking

Prepare for it. One executive I worked with was deathly afraid of public speaking early in her career. She decided to make progress slowly. One particular step she took was to come to every single meeting prepared with one or two points she would make. When she spoke up in the meetings, she sounded thoughtful, eloquent, and, ironically, spontaneous.

As you can tell from my cringeworthy story above, you *can* prepare for those situations. If you're attending a meeting or conference, ask yourself: "What is my goal for this meeting, and what would I like to say? Who is going to be there, and what issues might come up?" Jot down a few ideas and practice them out loud. Talk through these ideas with a colleague who knows the context. And if your job involves current events in any way, please check the news!

One executive I know regularly "cold-calls" people during her internal leadership meetings. If she's asked a question she doesn't have the answer to, then onstage in front of two hundred people she will point at someone in the audience and confidently ask, "Would you speak to that? I know you've been working on that issue." When my team and I coach her leadership team on their impromptu speaking, we always ask them, "What should you be prepared to say when your boss calls on you in the upcoming leadership meeting?"

Practice it. Practicing impromptu speaking is one of the most entertaining parts of our workshops. We do improv exercises to help people think and laugh on their feet. We ask people questions in front of the audience and have them respond in one minute or less. We give people random photos and ask them to give a persuasive speech inspired by that photo. Want to practice being unprepared? Partner up with a colleague and have them pepper you with questions and give feedback on your responses.

Take notes in the moment. When I go to a conference, I like to ask a question in nearly every session. It's a way to deepen my knowledge and also increase my networking contacts. As I sit in the audience and listen to a panel, I start to think of a question if I haven't already come prepared with one. I jot down a few notes and, when the moderator asks for audience questions, I raise my hand tall. I feel confident because I have the question written down right in front of me.

The PREP Formula

My favorite framework for public speaking, I learned from Toastmasters International and have used ever since. It's easy to learn and easy to use in nearly any professional or personal setting. It provides a quick framework for getting to the point and staying on point. It's called PREP, which stands for: Point, Reason, Example, and Point.

Point: Make one point. *I believe that . . .*

Reason: Provide an explanation of your belief. *And the reason I believe that is because . . .*

Example: Tell a story or anecdote that illustrates that point. *For example, just last week . . .*

Point: Conclude by restating your point. *And that is why I believe . . .*

Let's look at an example of PREP in response to the question *How do you feel about living in a big city?*

Point: I love living in a big city.

Reason: And the reason is because you can walk everywhere instead of driving.

Example: For example, last week I finally sold my car because my new office is a thirty-minute walk from my apartment. I get fresh air every single day.

Point: And that is why I love living in a big city.

Easy, right? You can use that framework for any subject, from talking about your favorite color to opining on multilateral trade negotiations.

Transition Phrases

You can also use a transition phrase to give yourself time to think of your answer. There are different types of transition phrases:

Summary: Thank you, I'd be happy to talk about my views on living in a big city.

Praise: You raised an important point.

Redirect: Actually, let me tell you why I hate living in a big city.

Bridge: We're not here to talk about cities, we're here to talk about the urban/suburban divide in our country.

These transition phrases help you transition from the question to your answer. They give you time to think, and they prepare your audience for your answer. When we discuss handling questions later in this chapter, we'll come back to these transition phrases.

You can use PREP without using the exact language "I believe" every single time, though it does provide guidance to keep you on track. Some of our clients work in environments where the words "I believe" are frowned upon, so they replace that language with "our view is," or they simply state their position without any preface.

You'll notice that the PREP framework works well for questions around belief and opinion, not questions like "What happened in the meeting last week?" For all other types of questions that PREP can't answer, there are a few points to keep in mind.

Develop an internal timer. When you speak off the cuff, pay attention to the passage of time. When we are unprepared, we tend to ramble as we constantly think of better ways to say the same thing. Develop an internal timer so that you become aware of when you've been talking for too long. If you feel you've been rambling, use "And that is why I believe" to restate your main point and quickly conclude.

Focus on one key message. When you speak off the cuff, you don't have time to list (or remember) multiple points. Choose one key message and then unpack it with an example. You can add a counterpoint as well to demonstrate multiple sides of an issue, but stick to one main message.

Come up with a few "go-to" stories or quotes. When speaking off the cuff, it can be helpful to have a few stories or quotes that you can easily refer to for inspiration. They should be relevant to the point you're trying to make and can help you fill time. What are your "go-to" stories? If you're the CEO of a company, maybe it's the company's founding. If you're the executive director of a nonprofit, maybe it's a success story of someone your organization has helped.

Here are a few delivery tips to keep in mind when speaking off the cuff:

Make eye contact. When thinking on your feet, your tendency is to look up and away or down at your feet while finding your words. It's okay to look away while thinking, but don't look away while talking. Your eye contact builds a connection with the audience and makes you look confident and purposeful. It's as important when speaking off the cuff as it is when giving a prepared speech.

Watch out for fillers. When you speak off the cuff, you'll tend to use more filler words because you are thinking of the next thing to say. Remember to *pause and breathe* instead, which makes you appear more thoughtful.

Watch out for nervous body language. The extra nerves you get from speaking off the cuff normally come out in your body language as well: repetitive hand gestures, playing with jewelry or clothing, or rocking back and forth. Use the breathing techniques you learned in Chapter 7 to calm your nerves and stand tall.

Smile! When you're nervous, you tend to withhold your smile while you concentrate on choosing your words. As long as it's appropriate to the conversation, let yourself smile while speaking. As we discussed in Chapter 6, a smile both makes you look more confident and makes you feel better.

How Do You Interrupt Someone?

This is a question I am often asked. A client will comment, "If I wait for someone to call on me, I'll never get a chance to speak!" Knowing *when* to speak up is just as important as knowing *how* to speak up.

Picture this: You're at a client meeting with a few of your colleagues. The client asks a question, and one of your colleagues starts to answer it, but you can tell that he has misheard the question. You observe the client pursing her lips with a slight frown on her face as she realizes she is not getting the information she needs. Your colleague is oblivious and continues talking. You silently think, "Are you kidding me?" and try to build up the courage to speak. In one week, two of my clients reported that exact same situation—and they weren't at the same meeting.

In some cultures, if you don't interrupt, you don't get a chance to speak. In other cultures, it can be interpreted as rude—especially if you are interrupting someone more senior than you. Here are some ways you can interrupt in a diplomatic way; adapt it according to your context.

> *Wait for the person speaking to take a breath*. He has to breathe sometime, right? When he breathes, jump in. A strategic filler word like "so" or "actually" can help you wedge yourself into the conversation.

> *Build or bridge.* Either compliment what the previous speaker said or bridge to a different direction, something like *I'm glad Steve brought that up*—or—*Let me build on what Steve said and come back to your original question.*

> *Be concise.* Keep it brief and concise; otherwise you wind up making the same mistake that Steve did. And remember to speak with a calm, confident attitude. Don't disparage Steve (though you may be doing so internally) and don't disparage yourself by second-guessing what you have to say.

Applying This Book to Impromptu Speaking

Everything you have learned so far in this book will help you with impromptu speaking. Recognize that impromptu speaking requires a few new skills, and practice using them every single day. The effect will be greater confidence in yourself and a more positive influence on others. Even impromptu speaking provides an opportunity to speak with impact.

Impromptu Practice. Find a colleague with whom to practice your impromptu speaking skills. Ask each other both fun and work-related questions, and try to keep your responses to one full minute, using PREP where appropriate. Provide feedback on how well the other person responded. And before each meeting or conference, come prepared with a few points you can make.

ANSWERING QUESTIONS FROM AN AUDIENCE

You've just delivered a beautiful speech or presentation. You spoke with passion and eloquence and inspired your audience. You concluded with a powerful call to action. But all of a sudden, you realize there's a question and answer (Q&A) session that you forgot about. So you look at your audience and stammer, *Um, so, you don't have any questions, right?*

Handling questions in front of an audience of any size—from a single client to a packed auditorium—can be a nerve-racking experience. Sometimes it's easier to just give the speech or presentation and go home. I'd like to make two main points about handling questions.

1. It doesn't have to be painful.

2. You don't have a choice.

Your willingness to answer questions reflects your openness and confidence about an issue and your relationship with the audience. In a meeting, if you just present your pitch and leave, you miss the opportunity to truly understand your client.

Imagine you're the leader of an organization and have a difficult message to impart. You have to make some painful budget cuts in the coming year. Some people in the audience will lose projects, and others will have to fire some of their direct reports. The audience is skeptical and anxious.

Which is better?

Option 1: You give your speech, explain the issue, and then get on your private jet and leave.

Option 2: You give your speech, explain the issue, and then say, "I'm going to stay here and take your questions, and I won't leave until every single question has been answered. We're a team, and we're going to get through this together." That is the kind of leader I want to be.

You may have to answer questions from clients or colleagues, from the board of directors, from members of the media, or from both supporters and detractors. Regardless of your industry, sector, or country, the more senior you become, the more people expect answers from you.

Preparing for Questions

There's a lot you can do to prepare for answering questions. The more you prepare, the more confident you will feel.

Research your audience. Find out as much information as you can about who will be in the audience. Ask the person who invited you, and speak to a colleague or friend who knows the industry or company. Ask yourself how people will feel about your subject; will they be excited about your message, or will they push back?

Research your field. Look at the latest developments in your field. Has a particular issue been in the news lately? Is there a controversy people are likely to ask about? Talk to your colleagues to hear what kinds of issues have come up in their own speaking engagements. See if your company has any guidance or talking points about how to handle certain issues. If you're the boss, recognize that your answers may *become* the talking points that others use going forward.

Research the context. Are you participating in a debate where someone else will refute your main points? Do you need to be prepared for pushback, either onstage or in the audience? Are you one of five companies presenting pitches to the same audience?

Identify your main messages. Remind yourself of the key messages in your speech or presentation so you can reinforce them later on in the Q&A session, especially if you have to bridge back to them.

Anticipate questions. You can anticipate at least 50 percent of the questions you'll receive in any setting. If you know the subject, the audience, and the reason they've invited you to speak, you'll know what types of questions they will ask. Practice answering those questions while referring back to your main points. Don't just focus on the easy questions; ask yourself which questions you hope you don't get, and practice answering them.

Role-play with a colleague. Have a colleague ask you questions and then provide feedback on how you answered. Talk through the answers to difficult questions to make sure you're conveying the right message. There have been times when I've practiced answering a question, only to say to myself: *Nope, I don't ever want to say that.*

Address potential questions in your speech or presentation.
If you're speaking to an audience that may push back on your
subject, address some of their arguments in the speech itself. It
won't eliminate all their questions, but at least you'll demonstrate
a balanced view in your speech.

Techniques When Taking Questions

Every time you speak in front of an audience, you have an
opportunity to build trust with them. How you answer their
questions plays a crucial role in the trust-building process. Do
you look defensive, or do you look open to engaging with others?
For my clients who give pitches, I recommend that they ask or
take questions *before* their pitch, so that the pitch addresses the
actual needs of their prospects. Dialogue builds more trust than a
one-way presentation.

If you give a speech right before taking questions from a large audience, conclude your speech and then confidently ask for questions.
Practice a phrase that feels natural to you, like:

And now, I'd love to take your questions.

I'm sure you have questions for me. What's on your mind?

Let me stop here. What questions do you have?

With a large audience, ask the questioner to stand up and identify
him- or herself. When someone stands up, it's easier for everyone in
the room to hear the question; and when you know which organization that person is from, it's easier for you to understand his or her
agenda.

Listen to the entire question, taking notes if necessary. You might
be tempted to nod while listening to the question. If you agree with
the questioner, that's fine. But if you don't agree, you should recognize
that—in an American context—you're still signaling agreement by
nodding your head.

Pause briefly before answering. Don't feel the need to rush into your answer. Use a transition phrase like the ones we discussed earlier in this chapter while you think of your answer.

Repeat the question out loud, rephrasing if necessary. Many times, the audience can't hear the question. This gives you time to think, and if it's a complicated or hostile question, you can rephrase it in a simpler and more neutral way.

Finally, answer the question concisely and confidently.

Handling a Hostile Question

The hostile questions are the ones that keep us up worrying the night before a speech or interview. Questions like:

Why didn't you take action sooner?

Didn't you know what the consequences would be of this decision?

What am I supposed to tell my family?

It's important to remain calm in these situations, even if the person asking the question is irate. You want to strike a balance of professionalism and empathy. I know, easier said than done, but it is crucial.

Try to rephrase the question in a neutral way that shows both sides of the issue. Let's say you work for a large university and are speaking at a community town hall to promote plans for a new building. You face serious pushback from community members who feel like you are taking over the neighborhood. You could rephrase a hostile question about expansion by explaining: *The question is about how we accommodate a growing number of students while respecting our neighbors who have lived here for generations.*

When you answer, address your answer to everyone in the room, not just the questioner. In that way, you continue to build a relationship with the entire audience, and you avoid creating a back-and-forth debate. When you've finished answering the question, call on someone else on the other side of the room. *Do not* go back to the hostile questioner and ask, "Did I answer your question?" You'll simply invite more debate.

How to Bridge

Those who speak to the media know the concept of bridging, when instead of answering a particular question, you bridge to another topic. You might have received a question you cannot answer or one that's irrelevant to your topic. Bridging is a useful tool, but be careful. If every speech is an opportunity to build trust with an audience, excessive bridging can damage the audience's trust in you. Here are some helpful phrases to be used sparingly:

That's not the issue; what we're really here to discuss is . . .

I think we're losing sight of the big picture, which is . . .

What I can say is this . . .

Once you use a bridging phrase, bring the conversation back to one of your main points. Have these phrases at the ready (and practice them in advance) so you feel confident when taking questions.

What If You Don't Know the Answer to a Question?

One concern people have is being asked a question they can't or won't answer. How you handle this question depends heavily on the context—are you in a meeting, or a media interview? As a general rule, if you don't know the answer to something, *don't make it up*. It ruins your credibility and can be dangerous to your organization.

In a presentation or meeting, it's absolutely legitimate to say: *That's a great question and I don't have that information right now. I'll get back to you tomorrow with an update*. Practice that sentence so you can say it with confidence and matter-of-factness, and it will be an important tool when answering questions. Many of my middle-management clients are afraid to say they don't know something, but their leaders will confide in me that they themselves say it all the time. Alternately, you could call on a colleague in the meeting who you think does have the right information.

During an interview, you could say, *I'm not in a position to answer that, but what I can say is this . . .*

If you have to push back on a question, you can use language such as:

I'm going to offer a counter to that argument.

Let me offer a different perspective.

Surprisingly, my experience has shown just the opposite.

If you need to calm an obstinate questioner, you can say, *I'd be happy to talk more with you about this one-on-one. Please come see me afterward and we can connect.* Your matter-of-factness when using these phrases keeps the conversation cool and calm instead of escalating into conflict.

What to Do After Taking Questions

Never end your Q&A session with the last question. If you do, your audience will leave with that random, unrelated question in their head and will have forgotten the main message of your speech. Rather, end with a strong restatement of your main message, something like, *I appreciate all your questions. Before you go, let me leave you with one final thought.*

In a meeting, you can end with a clear call to action.

After a Q&A session, you may be tempted to rush off, hide, and lick your wounds. Don't: you still have work to do. Stick around for those who would like to talk to you. It makes you look approachable and helps those in the audience who have questions but don't want to ask in front of a larger group. If, during your Q&A, you offered to follow up with someone, give them your business card and be available to them. You continue to build a relationship after the speech. Finally, remember to complete the post-speech debrief we discussed in Chapter 8.

Handling questions from an audience of any size is challenging. It requires more preparation and carries more risk than the speech itself, but it's critical for your reputation and credibility.

Q&A Prep. Before your speech, do your research and come up with a list of possible questions. Find a buddy to role-play the Q&A session and request feedback on how you respond. Don't forget to anticipate the tough questions and practicing bridging in your response or defusing the question. Practice responding within a one-minute time limit.

CHAPTER 11

Speak in Different Situations

On Calls, On Panels, or Across Borders

HANDLING CONFERENCE CALLS, WEB CONFERENCING, AND VIDEOCONFERENCING

The skills you've learned throughout this book apply to virtual speaking situations as well. As both technology and people's corresponding behavior evolve, visit www.speakwithimpactbook.com for updates and commentary and send us your experiences. 🌐 In each of the situations below, we'll cover tips for both content and delivery.

My colleague and fellow speaker Roger Courville, author of *The Virtual Presenter's Playbook* and chief content officer at webinar services firm EventBuilder, likes to remind people that a webinar doesn't replace an in-person conversation; it is simply an additional option for when you don't need to be there in person.[1] He says: "With any change of medium comes both loss and gain. The tradeoff between in-person and virtual is intimacy and impact versus reach. Don't think 'better or worse,' think 'it's just different.'"

Conference Calls (audio only)

Despite technological advances, voice-only calls aren't going away anytime soon. This section will cover conference calls but could just as easily cover a one-on-one phone call with your boss, your client, or an important influencer.

Content: A conference call is not usually the place for an inspirational "you can do it" type of speech, though any presentation is an opportunity to influence others. This is usually a medium for presenting information and checking for comprehension. As a result, clearly outline your content and include signposts that keep people focused. If the presentation is longer than ten minutes, stop periodically and give people time for questions. Be specific: *I'll stop here to see if you have questions . . . let's wait thirty more seconds in case someone has a question . . . if there are no questions, let's move on.* Speaking on a conference call can lead to awkward silences; but if you guide people through them, then you can make them more intentional.

When presenting on a conference call, I recommend having your notes in front of you. They can even be written word-for-word, as long as *you* wrote them in authentic, conversational language. Write in a reminder to take questions and to slow down. The more organized you are, the more logical your presentation will sound and the more effective you will be.

Delivery: Many people are relieved that no one can see their face on a call, but this makes them lazy when presenting. Actually, you have to be even *more* focused when speaking on a call. When no one can see your face, *all they can hear is your voice.* Our focus on voice and breathing in this book is critical here. Your energy and enunciation is key to demonstrating confidence and competency.

There are three things to keep in mind each time you speak on the phone, whether to one person or many:

1. *Stand up.* I'm serious. Stand up and wear headphones so you can use your hands. Standing and moving increases your en-

ergy and makes it easier to use breathing techniques that make your voice stronger.

2. **Smile.** I'm still serious. Smiling changes the way your voice resonates and makes it sound warmer and more confident. To your listener, it simply sounds like you are knowledgeable and confident.

3. **Slow down.** Because most of us are uncomfortable speaking to an audience we can't see, we rush to get through it as quickly as possible. This makes it hard for our audience to follow and, as a result, makes the presentation less effective.

If a local colleague or friend will also be joining the call, sit in the same room and, when it's your turn, present directly to them. Speaking to a smiling, nodding head can help your speaking feel more natural. Note: This only works if the listener is supportive, not if it's someone who brings the office energy down.

Web Conferencing (audio and video)

Webinars are another way to present information to a dispersed audience and record it for future use. Though some web conferencing is voice-only, oftentimes your audience can see you, even though you can't see them. This makes it even harder, because you have to look as conversational as if you were speaking to a live audience, but without the positive in-person feedback.

Content: My advice here is similar to what I recommend for conference calls: organize your presentation in advance and make sure it is easy to follow, paying attention to transitions and signposts. You might create a slide presentation that accompanies your video, but make sure you're not reading word-for-word what's on the slide. This is still an opportunity to create a relationship with your audience, so use language that's authentic to you and engages your audience.

Delivery: When you're on video, your audience can both see and hear you. Plan for that in advance by finding a well-lit place to sit, with a background that doesn't distract the audience. If you are in a noisy open office, find a quiet room. If you are at home, pay attention to the wall behind your computer to make sure it's professional. If you will be seated, dress professionally from the waist up (yes, you can actually wear pajama bottoms). Sit tall in your chair so you can use the breathing techniques you learned in Chapter 7.

Where should you look? Directly at the camera on your recording device, whether it's a computer, tablet, or other device. One unnatural factor in webinars is that you have to look "natural" while speaking to a piece of equipment. This isn't natural! That's why I practice my webinars in advance so I can become more comfortable speaking to the camera. Some people I know will hang up cute pictures of their families or pets next to the camera to help them relax.

And remember, as long as the webinar is running, act as if you were in front of an audience. You cannot get up and move around, adjust your clothing, or blow your nose without your audience seeing you.

Videoconferencing (two-way audio and video)

Enterprise-level solutions like Cisco's TelePresence let you have a life-like, interactive meeting with remote individuals. Many companies will use two-way videoconferencing for some of their most important internal conversations, from holding performance reviews to discussing new high-level strategies. While running a leadership communication program for the employees of one financial institution, I conducted ninety virtual coaching sessions in four months using TelePresence and learned quite a lot about the process.

Content: You might simply be attending a TelePresence meeting or preparing to present at one, but prior preparation is critical. Prepare exactly as you would when speaking in a meeting at the office: ask the Three Questions, structure your presentation, and dress as you would for an in-person meeting.

Delivery: In these videoconferences, you can see others and they can see you. Usually, you'll see a series of different screens showing you the other attendees, and when someone speaks, the software will increase their screen size so you can see them better. This software usually responds to sound, so be careful! If you sneeze, you'll be caught blowing your nose on the large screen. The same thing goes for your side conversations with others in your room. Use the mute button when you need to make noise discreetly. Remember to sit tall, breathe with purpose, and speak with a strong voice. All the elements of good delivery apply. And remember that as long as the videoconference is happening, you are "on" and people can see you. Act as if you were in the meeting room itself.

When we address a particular person while on videoconference, our instinct is to look at their image, wherever we see them on our screen (bottom left, top right, etc.). However, if we want them to see us looking directly at them, then we have to look into the camera. This can seem unnatural, and it is! But with practice you can become comfortable looking into the camera and trust that it will appear natural to your audience.

You can use videoconferencing for presentations as well as meetings. I once led a workshop at a firm in New York with twenty people in person and four groups of employees at four other locations in two countries joining remotely by video. During breakout sessions, the employees at each location did their own exercises. In this situation, my challenge was to both speak to the people in the room and still connect (and make eye contact) with the remote audience. If you bring handouts for the people in the room, send them *in advance* to the remote individuals. Solicit questions from those remote individuals as well, to create a shared experience with the group.

Remember that example I gave in Chapter 6 about leading a workshop for students in Nablus, in the Palestinian Territories, where a woman talked about the importance of a smile? We actually had eight students join us by videoconference from the Gaza Strip. I had to make sure that the small group felt included by soliciting their questions and even asking one of them to give an impromptu speech on video that all of us in Nablus could watch. While it wasn't as effective as having the students from Gaza in the room with us, we still provided a productive learning environment.

You can speak with impact on conference calls and through web conferencing and videoconferencing. Take the time to practice and become comfortable with the medium and you'll be able to maximize those opportunities.

SPEAKING ON OR MODERATING A PANEL

Outside of the office, one of the most common speaking opportunities you will have in the professional world is speaking on a panel. This is a different type of public speaking, for a few reasons. First, you are not alone. This fact is often enough to quell some of the nerves you feel preparing to speak! It could, however, become a new point of concern, especially if others on the panel are there to disagree with you. We'll deal with that a little later in this section.

When you speak on a panel, someone else is leading the conversation. Instead of giving a long, prepared speech, you are responding to the moderator's questions, interacting with the other panelists, and taking audience questions. It can be a very interactive format and a lively conversation.

It's a little easier to prepare for a panel because you don't need a thirty-minute presentation. You *do* need to prepare, though, and we'll cover how. Other benefits include the visibility and credibility that come with the occasion. Being a panelist builds you up as an expert or credible source on a subject. Imagine you work in a massive multinational corporation and are invited to speak on a panel at the annual conference. Now you are building a name within the entire company. If it's an external conference, there are usually online promotion, social media, and video associated with the event, which will build your reputation around the world.

How to Prepare for Being on a Panel

You prepare for a panel discussion just as you would for a speech or presentation. Start by asking the Three Questions: *Who is your audience? What is your goal? Why you?* In addition, there is a whole host of questions you'll want to ask the moderator, such as:

- What is the theme of the panel?

- Who else is on the panel?

- What questions will you ask us?

- What is the format of the panel?

- What is the physical setup?

- Do I need to prepare an opening statement?

Armed with this information, you can now prepare what to say. What are three messages you want to cover? Do you have any surprising anecdotes or statistics to share? Given the questions the moderator has sent over, how can you weave your main messages into your answers? Think about your goal from the Three Questions: What do you want people to do as a result of hearing you speak?

Think about what the other panelists might say. Will some disagree with you? There's nothing wrong with a healthy debate on a panel: in fact, it makes it more engaging. But if someone on the panel actively disagrees with your viewpoint, it's good to be prepared. One of our clients was invited to speak on a panel about women's reproductive rights, only to find out that she'd be debating a religious figure who vehemently disagreed with her methods. We worked together to prepare the talking points she would use.

When appropriate, connect with the panelists in advance, either by phone or online, so you start to build a collegial relationship with them. That warmth will come through on the panel.

Sometimes the moderator will ask you to prepare a short opening statement, perhaps about your background or area of expertise. This is a mini-speech, and you can prepare the same way you would for any other speech.

Once you've prepared your material, find a practice buddy and have them ask you questions. Our clients will come to us before a panel with a list of questions the moderator sent them, and we will help them prepare their answers. If the moderator hasn't sent over any questions in advance, we'll come up with the most likely questions and then send them to the moderator.

I remember speaking on a panel in Mauritius, a beautiful island country off the coast of Madagascar in southern Africa. The subject was leadership, and our moderator had sent us detailed questions in advance. I prepared using the methods we just discussed and arrived feeling confident and ready. Halfway through the panel, the moderator began asking us a new set of questions, and I was caught scrambling to respond. Later on, I checked my email and saw that, the evening before, she had sent us a new set of questions. Check your messages beforehand!

It's important to know what the physical setup of the room will be so you can choose the right attire. At a conference, panelists are usually seated, either in armchairs or high chairs. That means you need to choose attire that you can sit in comfortably. Ladies, if you wear a skirt, make sure the skirt is long enough that you are comfortable onstage. I've seen many women sit awkwardly in high chairs, attempting unsuccessfully to pull down their skirt while also trying to respond to the moderator's questions. One female executive I know always wears pants to a conference for just this purpose. Men should also pay attention to their posture: I've observed many men sit on a panel with their legs splayed wide open. When one person does it, others subconsciously imitate that same posture.

How to Speak on a Panel

The good and bad news about being on a panel is that you can sit down. It's more relaxing, but you can also forget that you're onstage. The moment you walk onstage, you are "on" and need to remain that way until you exit the stage. Even if you are not speaking, you are still in front of the audience. I once attended a "fireside chat" discussion where a journalist interviewed the former president of a university. The journalist sat up tall and was engaged and enthusiastic. The former president, by comparison, slumped in his chair and looked insolently at the floor. He had this gruff, bothered expression on his face and when he spoke, filler words punctured every sentence. To be fair, his content was spot-on and his ideas were enlightening, but I felt offended by his nonverbal communication.

When you speak on a panel, direct your answer to the entire audience. Make eye contact with individuals in the audience, just as you would in a speech or presentation. Keep your answers brief so that you don't monopolize the entire discussion. On a panel, I like to keep my responses to one or two minutes. If you don't have the answer to a specific question, then you can bridge back to one of your main messages. Build on a point one of the other panelists made to show continuity. Let it become an interactive, engaging conversation. It's okay to bring a notebook with you onstage to jot down notes. That can be helpful to capture ideas and refer back to them later.

After the panel, spend some time walking around the conference. This is the easiest type of networking, since people will come up to you. Think about what kind of connections you'd like to make at that conference, and have your business cards ready. We've worked with clients who were hoping to attract talented individuals to come work at their company, and after the panel they looked for potential new hires. If you were hoping for funding, be on the lookout for potential funders in the audience.

When You Are the Moderator

The role of moderator is critical in a panel discussion. It comes with all the visibility and credibility we discussed above, in addition to much more responsibility. If you are responsible for choosing speakers, think about who can offer different views on an issue so you don't have a group of people who all say the same thing. Which opinions need to be represented on an issue? Make sure you reach out to them well in advance, to invite them to speak.

Look at the list of panelists and determine your goals for this discussion. Ask yourself the Three Questions. Come up with a list of questions you want to ask the panelists, and plan to involve each person equally in the discussion. You might decide to ask each panelist the same questions, or create a different set of questions for each panelist.

As moderator, it's your responsibility to brief the panelists in advance, either by email or phone. Make sure they know of any time limits. Ask them how to pronounce their names, and practice in advance so you can comfortably introduce them onstage. You should also prepare your own opening statement to introduce the panelists and the discussion.

One major challenge I face as moderator is leading the discussion without dominating it. I see many moderators struggling with this when they want to add their own voice to the discussion—and in doing so, they take up the time of the panelists or of the audience.

Moderators, this is an important place for humility; it's not about you. You can prepare a brief introduction about your experience with the subject of the panel, but then sit back and prepare to play interviewer instead of expert.

Another challenge I see moderators struggle with is their energy level. When you are the moderator, your energy sets the tone for the entire panel, so it's crucial that you maintain an enthusiastic energy level. At one conference, I observed a moderator whose voice was so quiet that the other panelists had to lean in so they could hear her. They started to unconsciously mimic her voice. At one point, someone handed her a note while she was onstage. She read it and then said, "Apparently we've all been asked to speak up, so I'm wondering if you can all speak [whispering] *just a little bit louder.*" The irony was that after she whispered that request, everyone spoke even more softly.

A similar thing happened at another conference. This panel took place after lunch and was on a controversial topic, so it was critical that we keep people's energy up. I observed that the moderator and a few of the panelists were soft speakers. One of the panelists was someone I knew to be a strong, powerful speaker, but on this panel she started to speak with a quieter, more reserved voice. When I approached her after the panel to ask her about it, she acknowledged it. "I consciously lowered my energy to match the group so I didn't sound like a clown," she said. I told her that she could have *lifted up* the energy of the entire panel had she spoken in her natural voice. Our desire to fit in sometimes leads us to mimic the styles of others, but in this case everyone was bringing the room down.

Moderating a panel is like facilitating a meeting; you have to concurrently listen to the panelists and evaluate where you are in the flow of the panel. Has everyone spoken for equal amounts of time? Are you staying on topic? Do you still have time for audience questions? Your ability to stay focused and present is critical.

Start by welcoming the audience to the panel discussion. Introduce yourself and your background, the goal of the panel, and then provide a brief introduction of each panelist. Make this personal and authentic; don't simply read their bios. If you have a question about something in the panelists' bios, ask them in advance. Once you've given your introduction, you can call on the panelists in whichever order you prefer. Try to give each panelist an equal amount of questions and equal time to speak, since not every panelist will have the skill or comfort necessary to interrupt and make a comment.

I also highly recommend making time for audience questions. This is what engages the audience and makes sure you are addressing their questions. I've seen conferences in which there is purposefully no time for questions: it's simply a series of forty-five-minute panels, one after the other. While this is helpful to impart information, I believe it disregards the audience and their questions.

Once you make the decision to include time for questions, it is your job to ensure that there is enough time. You might have to interrupt a panelist who is speaking for too long, and you can do it in the interest of the audience by saying something like, *I'm going to jump in because I want to make sure we have enough time for audience questions.* If you find that the panel is running long and you had planned to ask your own questions, cut out your questions and turn it over to the audience.

When you turn it over to the audience, you can do a few things. You can ask for questions one at a time, or, if you are pressed for time, ask for three different questions and then let the panelists choose which questions to answer. Consider having someone in the room with a handheld microphone who can run over and give a mic to the person asking a question so everyone can hear it. If there is no mic present, then repeat the question out loud so the audience can hear it. If a questioner starts to make a prolonged statement, it's okay to gently interrupt that person and ask for the question. As the moderator, it's your job to protect the room, the entire audience, and the time limits you've set for the panel.

When you conclude, provide a few thoughts that summarize the discussion, and then send people on their way. Make it a clear transition so the audience can applaud. I once observed a moderator end a panel discussion and start to introduce the next speaker while the panelists were still onstage. Halfway through the introduction, he looked at the panelists and said, "You guys could stay up here or you could go, but you should probably go." I was thrown off by such a disrespectful conclusion.

Moderating and speaking on a panel are both terrific public speaking opportunities. Seek out those opportunities through your company or association memberships and use them to increase your public profile and your reputation.

SPEAKING ACROSS BORDERS

Preparing to Speak Abroad

These days, your audience rarely comprises one homogenous group. Even within a country, you have people of different ages, cultures, religions, and socioeconomic levels. Within an international organization like the World Bank, you could have people from fifty countries who all speak the same bureaucratic language but who have different cultural norms. Your challenge is to create a message that resonates with audience members of all kinds, especially if your speech could be posted online. There are some specific tips to keep in mind when you speak across borders.

Speaking outside your own country is an amazing opportunity for increased visibility, credibility, and sometimes even a brief vacation. In the past six years, I've given speeches or led training programs in: Israel, Argentina, South Africa, Northern Ireland, Uganda, the Palestinian Territories, Australia, Japan, England, and Mauritius—and hopefully there are many more destinations to follow. My goal is to help you develop a critical eye when preparing a speech for an international audience so that you can successfully translate that speech for different cultures.

When you ask the first of the Three Questions, *Who is your audience?*, ask if your content will resonate across borders. In the United

States, we tend to use a lot of sports analogies such as, *It was a home run*. I observed a colleague from New York include Yiddish expressions that not everyone in the audience could understand. Depending on your industry and which city you live in, you could hear golfing terminology or Spanish during a presentation. I was teaching a workshop in Sydney, Australia, for a group of women leaders from the Asia Pacific region when an American colleague presented something simple by saying, *It's a piece of cake!* I'm not sure our audience members understood the reference.

In Chapter 4, we talked about humor and warned that it might not carry across borders. Talk through your humor with the person who invited you to speak and make sure it will have the intended effect. What's acceptable humor in one country may not be acceptable in another. Phrases and jokes are a few challenges we face when speaking across borders. Attitude is another. In Japan, it's a sign of humility to apologize when you start a speech, but to an American audience it will sound unprofessional.[2]

Test your speech out on people who represent your target audience to see if your message resonates. Research the culture thoroughly so you get a feel for its dynamics. Ask for guidance on attire so you don't unintentionally offend your audience before you even say a word. Research cultural norms of touch so you don't start off on the wrong foot (pun intended) when you try to shake someone's hand. And speak to people on the ground to make sure you're not using outdated stereotypes.

As I said earlier in this section, we are always speaking to a diverse group of some sort, even within our country's borders. All of these techniques can apply whether you're speaking to a different line of business within your organization or speaking in a foreign country.

Giving Speeches While Traveling

Do not, if at all possible, give a speech on the same day you arrive in a foreign country. Even if you are one of those lucky few who can sleep on flights, and even if you fly business or first class, I recommend taking at least one day to acclimate to a new climate and a new time zone. Give yourself at least one night to sleep in a real bed, and plan on time for travel or weather delays. I normally plan some sightseeing activities for that first day.

If your speech is relatively soon after you arrive, pack your speech attire in your carry-on. I can't count the number of times I've seen colleagues present in the casual clothing they flew in because their luggage was lost along the way. Bring snacks with you that you can rely on right before you speak. While I *love* trying new foods and will often eat anything in front of me, before a speech I want to know that whatever I eat will not interfere with my stomach when I go onstage. Drink lots of bottled water, since traveling can dehydrate you.

When you learn about the culture of the country you're going to be speaking in, learn how to say "good morning" in that language. When I travel, I like to introduce myself to the audience by saying, *in their language,* "Good morning, my name is Allison Shapira, and I don't speak [local language]." From Austria to Japan, that line always gets laughs from the audience and shows respect for their language.

If you're speaking to a group of people who have varying levels of fluency in that language, make sure you slow down and enunciate clearly, especially if your remarks are being simultaneously interpreted. If possible, walk through your remarks in advance with the interpreter to make sure he or she feels comfortable translating not just the words but also the intent behind the words. If you have multiple speeches in a country, see if you can work with the same interpreter.

Every time we speak, we pick up on people's body language. But in another country, body language is culturally dependent. If people look serious, it could simply be a sign of respect, or they could be concentrating to understand you. Don't look for the same visual cues you'd look for in your own country. Speak with the organizer of your event in advance so you know what to expect.

Traveling for public speaking is one of the joys of my career. A lifelong adventurer, I look for any excuse to visit a new country and connect with people through communication. Remember that trip to Mauritius I referenced earlier in this chapter? I was there to visit a friend who had just formed a new political party. I was able to lead a public speaking workshop for that new party, giving me an insight into the country I would never have had as a tourist. Getting to know a country while speaking is a wonderful way to connect with others and see just how similar we all are.

SPEAKING IN A FOREIGN LANGUAGE

Many of my clients speak English as a second (third, fourth, or fifth) language. I myself have given speeches in Italian and Hebrew (and once in Arabic, but it wasn't very good). Many of you reading this book will not have a choice; you already live and work in a specific country and are simply expected to speak publicly in that language. But some of you will have the option of deciding which language to speak.

Speaking to an audience in their language is an incredible form of respect for their culture, and a way to connect with them on a deeply personal level. In some countries, there is the language of the government and the language of the people; it sends a powerful message when you speak the language of the people.

As an American, I have always tried to disprove the stereotype that people from the United States don't speak a foreign language (many of us speak several!) or that they expect everyone else to speak English. Watch the first few minutes of Facebook CEO Mark Zuckerberg's Q&A at Tsinghua University in China.[3] Don't listen to what he says (unless you understand Mandarin Chinese), but focus solely on the audience's reaction, which is surprise and delight.

Regardless of which foreign language you are speaking, here are some important tips to keep in mind:

- *Speak that language as much as possible beforehand.* Watch TV, listen to the radio, and talk to yourself out loud in that language so that it feels natural. When I'm preparing to speak in a foreign language, I make myself *think* in that language so that it becomes my default language instead of English.

- *Prepare the exact phrases in advance.* When you speak a foreign language in front of an audience, it's hard to think of the right words on the spot. It's much easier to think of those words in advance. You don't have to memorize them, but take the time to find the right phrases and practice them out loud so they come more easily when you present.

- *Choose words that are comfortable to you.* In any language, there are words that are difficult to pronounce. If you find yourself stumbling over a word while practicing, you will probably stumble over the word in front of the audience. Take the time to find words that are familiar to you.

- *Bring notes.* It's okay to bring notes with your outline and key phrases so that you don't have to remember them on the spot. You can glance down to remember a phrase and then smoothly keep going. Practice giving the speech or presentation from those notes so you can refer to them easily.

- *Practice with a native speaker.* Run through your speech in advance with a native speaker of that language. This helps ensure that your words and argument make sense, and also lets you talk through any language questions.

- *Slow down and enunciate.* When you are nervous, you tend to rush. Add to that a foreign accent, and it will be hard for people to understand you. There's nothing wrong with having a foreign accent; simply make sure you slow down and enunciate so people can follow you.

- *Pause and breathe.* In my experience, non-native speakers are more likely to use filler words like *um* or *ah* while thinking of the next thing to say, oftentimes translating in their head right in front of the audience. As you go from one sentence to the next, *pause and breathe* instead, and you'll sound more purposeful.

- *Don't be perfect!* Foreign language speakers tend to be their own worst critics. They expect their speech to be perfectly grammatical, which is *impossible*. Not even native speakers speak with perfect grammar. When you relax the need for perfection, it lets you focus on your message and your audience instead of on your language. A caveat: this does not apply to slides or handouts. If you are printing slides or handouts in a foreign language, have a native speaker proofread them to make sure they are grammatically correct.

I have so much respect for people who speak publicly in a foreign language. Use the above tips to excel in any situation.

CHAPTER 12

Build Your Executive Presence

Five Components to Bring Out Authority and Authenticity

DEFINING EXECUTIVE PRESENCE

I remember the first time I heard about executive presence. Clients would mention it when we discussed their public speaking goals. They'd say things like, "I'd really like to build my executive presence so I can own the room," or their bosses would send them to my workshops and tell me, "They need to build their executive presence if they want to get promoted in this company."

There are some terrific books on the subject, from *Executive Presence: The Missing Link Between Merit and Success* by Sylvia Ann Hewlett to *The Power of Presence: Unlock Your Potential to Influence and Engage Others* by Kristi Hedges. ⊕

Many of the components of executive presence are actually best practices of public speaking, such as: how to speak with confidence, connect with an audience, and command a room. As a result, I've developed my own methodology for teaching executive presence based on how I teach public speaking and based on my experience building *stage presence* as a performer.

Throughout this book, you have been building your executive presence. You are developing a way of speaking and acting that makes others take notice and listen.

In this chapter, I'll cover what I believe to be the five components of executive presence, and I'll point to where you can read in the book to more intentionally build them. You will find that we have covered many of them already.

I discovered the power of *stage presence* when I was fifteen years old. As a sophomore at Booker High School in the visual and performing arts program in Sarasota, Florida, I once auditioned for a performance troupe that toured through our campus. During the audition, ten of us lined up in front of an auditorium full of students. One by one, we stepped forward and simply stated our name. No explanation, no bio, just our name. When my time came, I walked forward, then paused and breathed. I looked calmly and purposefully around the room and felt a sense of anticipation as the audience waited for me to speak. Then I slowly and clearly stated my name as if it were the most critical piece of information that someone should know about me. I made it into the troupe.

Later on, when explaining why we were chosen, the troupe director would point to my introduction—not my name, but how I had pronounced my name—as the reason I was chosen. At the time, he had no idea that I was an opera singer in training or that I had performed in front of thousands of people. It all came across in those two words.

Think about what gives an opera singer *stage presence*: it's the way the soprano walks purposefully out onstage, her passion for the music; it's the tenor's confidence in his craft after years of study and practice. It's the deep connection they both feel to the material, to the music, to *why* they do what they do. They don't rush through their arias; they take their time and focus on the experience of their audience. They own the stage and believe in their right to be there.

Now I'd like you to imagine someone with *executive presence*: perhaps the CEO of your organization, perhaps a member of the board, perhaps one of your colleagues without formal authority or a fancy title. It could be the confident way she walks into the room and starts a meeting. It might be the clear, decisive way he speaks, cutting out the jargon and getting straight to the point. Perhaps it's the reputation he has within the organization. Maybe it's in the power of her voice. All those attributes are critical elements of executive presence, and together they command your audience's attention.

A few years ago, I was preparing to give a keynote on executive presence to a group of banking executives in a Fortune 50 company. Before my program, I interviewed three different leaders in the firm. I asked them why executive presence was important when presenting to clients. Their responses were incredibly illuminating: "Do you look like you deserve to be there? Does what you say make sense? Do you look like you'll be able to execute the business? Your executive presence does a lot of the talking."

It's not about creating a false leadership persona—your audience can see right through that, and it negatively affects your reputation and credibility. Presence requires you to connect authentically with what drives you in your work, and then allows that sense of purpose to infuse your words, your actions, and your energy.

As you'll see below, the five components of executive presence build off each other—developing one will help develop the others. And conversely, a lack of one will usually diminish the others. They are not talents; they are a selection of skills that you can build and develop over time.

Executive presence does not come from your title; it comes from how you handle yourself. I've seen CEOs with no presence, and I've seen college students with a powerful presence. You can feel it in person or over the phone.

It's also highly cultural. My colleague Jeanine Turner, an associate professor at Georgetown University, describes presence as a social construct. That means it's based on expectations and assumptions of how people should act, and in this chapter we'll talk about how to balance those expectations with what's authentic to you.

Much of the research on executive presence has focused on an American business context, but you can observe it in people all over the world. The five components I describe below don't change according to your culture, but *how you use them* can change according to cultural norms and expectations.

As you read through each component, make a note of where you are strongest and where you would like to improve; there are tips to help you at the end of each section. The five components of executive presence are:

1. Content

2. Confidence

3. Nonverbal

4. Voice & Tone

5. Interactions with Others

1. CONTENT: KNOW YOUR STUFF

The first component of executive presence is knowing what you're talking about. If you're giving a speech or speaking up in a meeting, it's demonstrating that you know your subject and have a clear point of view.

But it doesn't simply mean being an expert. Can you think of someone in your organization who knows everything about a subject, but you would never put him or her in front of an audience? This is where technical people have an "a-hah" moment. It's not about rambling endlessly in technical jargon while your audience is tuning out. It's about being able to articulate a clear, decisive message without jargon or generic business language. It's about getting to the point and having the courage to speak *up* when the stakes are high, keeping your voice calm while others around you are losing their heads.

Imagine sitting in a boardroom while someone in the room proposes a new project. As that person speaks, your emotional intelligence guides you to look around and observe people fidgeting uncomfortably in their chairs and visibly wincing while this person speaks. You know exactly why this project won't work, and you have the feeling that everyone in the room is thinking the same, but no one has the guts to say it. You don't have the formal authority to stop the project, but still you believe something has to be said. You *pause and breathe*, gather your thoughts, and then calmly speak up, suggesting that the speaker solicit feedback from people on the ground before making a decision. You notice the tension in the room dramatically release.

Your ability to influence the course of a meeting is part of your executive presence.

Here are some tips to work on this component:

- *Be prepared.* You can't walk into these situations and expect to have an impact. Prepare for every meeting by asking the Three Questions we discussed in Chapter 2 so you come prepared with a point of view. Bring power questions to ask, to keep people on track.

- *Get to the point.* You'll remember Chapter 5, where we discussed how critical it is to be concise when you speak. In fact, in many industries, your higher-ups will assess your leadership potential based in part on your ability to speak concisely and deftly lead a conversation. Learn how to make your speech more concise based on techniques in Chapter 5, and practice your impromptu speaking skills from Chapter 10.

- *Lose the jargon and fillers*. You can't inspire through jargon; you inspire through descriptive, authentic language. Let yourself use language that's conversational and genuine to you, and keep out the fillers and overly casual phrases like "you guys."

- *Speak up when others are afraid to do so.* Let your sense of conviction guide you to speak up when you know it's important. If you are nervous about speaking up, review Chapter 7 to help you *pause and breathe* and find your courage to speak.

- *Know when* **not** *to speak.* Building this component of your executive presence will cause you to speak up more often—which is generally a positive change—but I want to caution you to be judicious about it. Your executive presence doesn't come from hogging the airtime on a conference call or in a meeting; it comes from being strategic about *when* you speak up and *what* you say. It also means deciding when something is better left to a one-on-one conversation than a group debate. As one of my executive clients says, "Sometimes the person who speaks the *least* in the meeting has the most power."

2. CONFIDENCE

The confidence component of executive presence is bigger than simply knowing your subject or being prepared. If that were the case, then over-preparing would be the key to confidence.

As we learned from Chapter 7, confidence comes from many factors, only one of which is knowing your subject. In addition, do you truly believe in what you are saying? Do you believe in what you represent? Are you proud of the work you do?

Confidence comes from a belief in yourself, in your subject, and in the value of the work you do. It's an aura that surrounds what you say and how you say it. It comes across over the phone or in person.

One of my mid-career graduate students was preparing for a job interview for a senior role with one of the biggest technology companies in the world. She confided in me that she still wasn't sure she would get the job, and she even believed that they were going to give her a verbal *rejection* during the final in-person interview. But she also stated how strongly she believed that she was the right person for the job and gave me compelling reasons why. As she listed those reasons, her voice strengthened and she sat up tall. She started to own her confidence in herself. We decided that she would visualize the upcoming job interview in advance and then walk in with the mind-set that she was *going* to get the job. One week later, she emailed me that she got the job.

When you believe in yourself and in what you represent, you give off an energy that others pick up on immediately. It doesn't have to be loud or brash; it can be a quiet but assured sense of confidence. It's a sense of conviction in yourself and your abilities. Of all the components of executive presence, I find confidence to be the most powerful, because it breathes life into everything else.

Here are some tips to speaking with confidence:

- *Ask yourself* Why you? *to connect with your sense of purpose.* Talk through your *Why you?* with a friend or colleague to identify what motivates you in your work. If you can't find it in your job, look for it in your life overall. Use the *Core Value Statement* exercise in Chapter 7 and speak it out loud before you walk into a room.

- *Use mental rehearsal to visualize your success.* Visualizing the scenario in your mind is an effective way to build up your confidence in any situation, from a one-on-one difficult conversation to a stressful All Hands meeting.

- *Look for allies.* Find those people in your work and in your community who build you up and see your potential. Spend time with these people to build up your confidence.

- *Do your homework.* While preparation is not the only indicator of confidence, it's a big one. Make time in your day to prepare for those situations.

3. NONVERBAL

When you walk onstage or into a conference room, every part of you is communicating: your eyes, your body, and your attire. All these components have a significant impact on your executive presence. When speaking, it's important to make sure that everything is *saying the same thing*.

Many times, people's body language will betray their nervousness or lack of confidence. Their fidgeting hand gestures will undermine the clear recommendations they're making. Pacing back and forth will make them look restless and unfocused when they need to be fully present. Chapter 6 taught us techniques to handle this.

At the Harvard Kennedy School, there is a postgraduate fellowship that brings U.S. military officers (and some civilians) to the campus for one year. These senior leaders audit classes, conduct research, and provide a valuable perspective on campus based on their military experience. These fellows do not dress in military uniform, but I can still identify them from across the room. Why? Because of how they carry themselves: their posture, their pace, and, for some, their military haircut. Their executive presence comes across in their nonverbal communication.

Here are a few tips to build your nonverbal presence:

- *Pay attention to how you enter a room.* Center yourself before you walk into a room to make sure you are purposeful and intentional. When you're standing, stand tall on two feet and avoid nervous fidgeting. When you're seated, let yourself take up space as opposed to crossing your arms and shrinking.

- *Make eye contact.* Eye contact demonstrates your confidence to speak and builds trust with your audience. Especially when you are speaking up about something important, make eye contact with the people you want to take action.

- *Use hand gestures that are purposeful, instead of ner-vous.* Nervous fidgeting or pacing will make you look unpre-pared and detract from your executive presence. Using the techniques we discussed in Chapter 6, practice gestures that match the language you use.

- *Be strategic about what you wear.* Your attire communi-cates with your audience in different ways. It can show profes-sionalism or laziness. It can show national pride or a lack of caring. I can't tell you what to wear, but I can tell you to understand what your attire communicates, and to dress in the way that you'd like to be perceived. A wrinkled shirt, chipped polish on your fingernails, and unbrushed hair can reduce your executive presence because it makes you look like you don't care.[1] It's not about wearing a suit in every situation, although there is fascinating research that shows the *perceived* authority that comes with wearing a suit can make you more influential.[2] What you wear sends a message, whether it's choosing *or refusing* to wear a suit.

4. VOICE & TONE

Does the power of your voice match the power of your words? When you speak, do you sound like you believe in what you are saying? Your tone of voice can stop someone in their tracks or entice them to lean in and listen. That's important any time you speak in public, and it's particularly important when you build your executive presence.

Imagine that you're on an airplane that's experiencing turbulence. It starts out as just a couple of bumps but soon progresses to such an extent that even the frequent flyers are looking at each other with raised eyebrows. Everyone double-checks their safety belts and then grips their armrests firmly. This is when I practice purposeful breathing. Suddenly, you hear the pilot's voice over the intercom.

What are you listening for in the pilot's voice? You're listening for calm and reassurance. You're listening for professionalism and competence. For me, all of that comes across in the first three words the pilot says: "Ladies and Gentlemen." I can hear it in the even pacing of the words and the calm tone of voice that says everything is going to be okay.

We spent a significant amount of time in Chapters 6 and 7 looking at how your voice can convey confidence or doubt. The moment you speak, your tone communicates before the words even sink in. And if there's a disconnect between the words and the tone, people will believe the tone. When they speak in public, most people focus on the words and assume the tone will happen naturally; it doesn't necessarily.

Everything you have learned about breathing and voice will enhance your executive presence, and the confidence you built in learning these skills will calm your nerves and let your voice convey the full strength of your conviction.

Here are a few tips to keep in mind:

- *Practice purposeful breathing*. Take time to *pause and breathe* before you speak. It grounds you, gives you time to reflect on your words, and makes you appear (and sound) more thoughtful.

- *Speak with a clear, unrushed voice.* When you connect with your confidence and conviction in what you do, it comes across in the strength of your voice. It's not about yelling, it's about speaking clearly and confidently, without mumbling or rushing.

- *Practice the pause.* Remember that story I told in the beginning of the chapter about demonstrating executive presence by only stating my name? It wasn't only my name that commanded attention; it was the pause and eye contact that I used before stating my name, combined with the strength of my voice when I spoke. Taking the time to pause in front of an audience shows that you are comfortable with silence and causes people to lean in and listen.

- **Watch out for uptalk and vocal fry.** The vocal ticks we discussed in Chapter 6 are particularly harmful to your executive presence, as they can make you sound unsure or lazy. Let your cadence rise and fall naturally.

5. INTERACTIONS WITH OTHERS

Throughout this book, I stress that public speaking is a way to build a relationship of trust with your audience. It's also an integral part of your executive presence. It comprises your relationships with others, your reputation, and your integrity.

Your presence isn't something you put on and take off like a jacket; it's something you build with every single interaction. When you walk into a meeting, do others view you as a trustworthy partner? When you walk into a room or pick up a phone, your reputation precedes you. Sometimes you are in the meeting because of your reputation. Sometimes, you are in the meeting *despite* your reputation.

I'm sure you can think of someone who has a powerful voice, or confident body language, or flawless command of their subject—but you can't trust them. Or perhaps you don't trust the organization they represent. If you are all talk but no action, then it reduces your executive presence. Presence is not just about how you speak or act; it's about how you make others feel.

Here are a few tips for improving those relationships:

- **Be physically present with others.** When you interact with others, are you focused, or distracted? Put aside your digital device or turn off notifications and be fully present with someone. Make direct eye contact, practice active listening, and focus solely on that person.

- **Be accessible.** If no one can get on your calendar and you don't respond to emails, then you build a wall around yourself that prevents you from connecting with others. Make time to walk around and speak with people, and be available when others need to talk.

- **Live your values.** You set a strong example for others when you live the values you espouse. That's why the Core Value Statement is such a powerful tool, as it helps you identify those values and think about how you live them with consistency. Recognize that you can serve as a role model every single day.

- **Ask for feedback.** Soliciting feedback from others—colleagues, managers, or friends—is a powerful way to build relationships and also a valuable way to develop self-awareness. In her book *The Power of Presence,* Kristi Hedges encourages people to complete a presence audit as a way of soliciting feedback from trusted colleagues[3] and friends.

Each of the five components of executive presence calls on skills we have built so far in this book. Each time you speak, you have an opportunity to impact people's behaviors and influence their actions. By focusing on your executive presence, you ensure that every aspect of your communication delivers the same powerful message.

Read through the five components of executive presence and evaluate yourself on each one on a scale of 1 to 5. Use the Executive Presence Self-Assessment available at www.speakwithimpactbook.com. Look at the lowest-rated categories and read through the tips above to address them.

CHAPTER 13

Find Your Courage to Speak

How to Use This Book to Speak Up

USING THIS BOOK

Where do you go from here? I hope this book has inspired you to look inward to determine why you are called to speak. I hope it has given you the courage to seek out more speaking opportunities at work or in your community, and to use your voice to have an impact on the world around you. And I hope that you take action based on your words.

Review all the speaking opportunities described in Chapter 1 and make a commitment to find one speaking event in the coming month. Then, seek out another one. The more you apply these skills, the faster you will build your skills and see improvement.

If you haven't found a practice partner to go through the book with, find one now and use this person as a trusted advisor to help you apply what you learned.

This book is filled with tips and techniques, but where do you start once you have a speech on your calendar?

When You Have Two Hours or Less to Prepare a Speech

We've all been in the situation where we have to prepare a speech with thirty minutes' to two hours' notice. In that case, look at the sidebar

"How to write a speech in thirty minutes" and spend as much time as you can practicing and using the practice methods we discussed in Chapter 5.

When You Have One Week to Prepare a Speech

You can also use the sidebar "How to write a speech in thirty minutes," but now add in the polishing component from Chapter 5.

When You Have One Month to Prepare a Speech

Read this book with your upcoming speech in mind.

Use Chapter 2 to ask the Three Questions and determine the main message of your speech.

Use Chapter 3 to walk you through the writing process.

Read Chapter 4 for ideas to connect with your audience through persuasion, stories, or humor.

Use Chapter 5 to polish and practice your speech.

Use Chapter 6 to add engaging delivery tools.

Chapter 7 will calm you down and help you center yourself.

Chapter 8 will prepare you for being in front of an audience.

For more specific situations, look at Chapters 9, 10, and 11 to help you prepare. At the end of nearly every chapter, there are exercises to help you apply the learning. You can go from one exercise to the next to continue building your skills.

HIGHLIGHTING COMMON THEMES

I started out as an opera singer, performing the works of others before I had the courage to write my own songs as a folk singer. I now believe that both opera and folk music have much to teach us about public speaking. While opera teaches us the techniques and discipline to build our skills, folk music teaches us the power of authenticity over perfection.

In this book, I've given you a process for many of the common public speaking opportunities, from day-to-day presentations to career-changing speeches. There will undoubtedly be updates as technology changes and as our understanding of human behavior changes. I myself am constantly learning new techniques and strategies from colleagues and clients around the world. Visit www.speakwithimpactbook.com for new tools and to read the experiences of others who have used this book successfully. ⊕ Send us your feedback so we can share it with others.

I'd like you to keep in mind some important themes that I've weaved in throughout this book:

- *Public speaking is a skill, not a talent.* My teaching philosophy rests on the belief that each one of us can be a powerful public speaker with practice and feedback. The more you use this skill and the more you focus on making progress, the better you become.

- *Public speaking is something we do every single day.* From phone calls to webinars, presentations to meetings to town halls, we have daily opportunities to speak in public. It can happen anywhere in the world, at every stage in our career, no matter our background.

- *We all get nervous.* If you feel nervous before a presentation, remember that you are not alone. The fear of public speaking is universal, and most people will sympathize with you. Remember that everyone in the audience wants you to do well.

- *It's about being authentic, not perfect.* Nobody wants to hear a perfect speech or presentation; they want to feel that the speaker is authentic and genuinely cares about his or her subject. Forget the need to be perfect and you'll reduce a lot of your stress.

- ***It's about connecting with your audience and building trust.*** Giving a speech or presentation is an opportunity to build a relationship of trust with your audience, whether it's one person or a thousand people. The tools in this book will help you focus on your audience and your message in a way that connects on a personal level.

- ***It's about exercising leadership with your voice.*** Professor Marshall Ganz says, "Mobilizing others to achieve purpose under conditions of uncertainty—what leaders do—challenges the hands, the head, and the heart."[1] Once you determine what you want to say, it's about finding a way to mobilize others to act.

BUILDING ALLIES AROUND YOUR IDEAS

Throughout this book, I've referenced the importance of speaking up, even if you are afraid to do so. Speaking in public comes with certain dangers. What you say may be politically or culturally dangerous. Speaking up may bring with it *physical* danger based on what you have to say or whether cultural expectations allow you to speak. You might be a new political figure speaking out against the current system's corruption or a young woman speaking out against dangerous cultural practices in your community. I've met women who had the courage to speak publicly about their rape in order to change the public taboo in their country and give other women the courage to confront their attackers. When we speak out about things that challenge society's norms, there is danger in our words.

The last thing I'd want you to do is read this book and give a speech that puts your life in danger. When you ask the Three Questions

(*Who is your audience? What is your goal? Why you?*) you'll have a sense of whether or not your speech will be controversial. If you believe your message will be dangerous, take steps to build allies along the way. Find people—in your political party, in your organization's leadership, in your community—who support you and will be willing to support you publicly. Build up those allies so that when you do speak, you don't have to speak alone.

At the same time, don't just seek out those who think like you. Reach out to those who disagree with you so you can better understand their point of view. You might do this in order to better address their issues, or perhaps adjust your own view. Unfortunately, we have a tendency to accept comments that already support our worldview and discredit those that push back, leading to a dangerous mind-set that can't accept opposing viewpoints. Have the courage to listen to others, and have the humility to accept that you may be wrong.

From a more practical perspective, finding allies to help you with your public speaking is a critical part of your success. In all of our workshops, participants speak and receive feedback from their peers. Oftentimes that feedback is richer and more nuanced than I could give, because those peers know the subject matter better than I do. The friendships that emerge from those workshops continue to this day, as people call on each other to practice their most important speeches and presentations. The process of asking for and receiving feedback creates a powerful bond with others, as you are willing to look vulnerable in front of them. Find allies who can give you honest feedback on your speaking strengths and where you can improve.

LISTENING TO OTHERS

This entire book has focused on the art of speaking up, which makes it easy to forget the importance of listening.

Listen to your audience members and their needs before you draft your remarks. Who will you be addressing, and what is important to them?

Listen to how your audience reacts to your remarks in the moment. What is their body language saying and, when they ask questions, what are they really saying? In a meeting, listen to those around you instead of simply thinking of what to say next.

Listen to the views of others, even when you don't agree with them. In the United States, we are fiercely proud of our First Amendment right that protects the freedom of speech, a freedom I wholeheartedly embrace. With that right comes a great responsibility because *our words matter*. With our words, we can build someone up or tear them down. We can monopolize air time with our beliefs, or we can respect other people's right to speak.

Listen to your own inner voice and acknowledge what you truly want to say, not just what you think others want to hear. When you feel an ethical conflict between what your organization tells you to say and what you feel is right, listening to this inner voice may cause you to rethink what to do with your life.

Know When Not to Speak

I learned a humbling lesson during one of my leadership courses in graduate school. We walked into the classroom one day to find that a group of students had written six student names on the board along with the words "Today, could these people please refrain from speaking and leave some air for the rest of us?" My name was one of the six written on the board. I was shocked and embarrassed. I liked speaking up in class because the subject interested me and I believed I had an important perspective to offer my peers. But after consulting with a few friends from the class, I learned that my behavior was predictable. Whenever there was a challenge or question thrown out to the group, I would jump in with the answer before others had had time to grapple with it. I became a crutch for others.

You no doubt have something to contribute in nearly every situation. As a result of reading this book, you may feel particularly emboldened to do so, but remember to do so strategically. If you constantly speak up and monopolize the meeting, you are taking away other people's time to speak and grapple with challenges. As the Dalai Lama says, "Sometimes one creates a dynamic impression by saying something, and sometimes one creates as significant an impression by remaining silent."[2]

ENDING WITH A CALL TO ACTION

I believe that each of you has something powerful to say—on behalf of yourself, your organization, or your community. Public speaking is about finding your own voice, building your communication skills, and finding your courage to speak. It's about recognizing what's important to you and what needs to be done in the world, then mobilizing others to address it—from a new corporate strategy to a vision of social change. That is how you exercise leadership with your voice.

On March 24, 2018, during the March for Our Lives in Washington, DC, volunteers were handing out posters along 7th Street NW. One poster showed a group of people, one shouting into a megaphone, and the word ACT! in big red letters across the top. I was struck by the correlation between speaking and acting. You could look at that sign and say, "Well, they're just speaking; they're not actually taking action." But in fact, speaking up is the first step to taking action. Because when you speak up about an issue, you start to take ownership of the solution. Gordon Whitman, author of *Stand Up! How to get involved, speak out, and win in a world on fire,* says that you go from being a passive member of society to an agent of change.[3]

My call to action is that you use these skills for good and not for evil.

For centuries, dictators and despots have used public speaking to divide people instead of bringing them together. Recognize the incredible power that comes from the spoken word, and use it to create community, connection, and trust. We need this in business, we need this in politics, and we need it in the world at large. When you use these skills for good, you will have a powerful and positive impact on the world around you.

Endnotes

Introduction

1. *Toastmasters International*—Home, www.toastmasters.org. Accessed 21 Feb 2018.

Chapter 1

1. Pentland, Alex "Sandy." "Defend Your Research: We Can Measure the Power of Charisma." *Harvard Business Review*, Feb. 2010, hbr.org/2010/01/defend-your-research-we-can-measure-the-power-of-charisma. Accessed 21 Feb 2018.
2. Pentland, Alex "Sandy." "The New Science of Building Great Teams." *Harvard Business Review*, Apr. 2012, hbr.org/2012/04/the-new-science-of-building-great-teams. Accessed 21 Feb 2018.
3. *Toastmasters International*—Home, www.toastmasters.org. Accessed 21 Feb 2018.
4. Toastmasters International® and all other Toastmasters International trademarks and copyrights are the sole property of Toastmasters International. This book is the opinion of the authors and is independent of Toastmasters International. It is not authorized by, endorsed by, sponsored by, affiliated with, or otherwise approved by Toastmasters International.
5. *TEDx Program*—Home, www.tedx.com. Accessed 21 Feb 2018.
6. *TED: Ideas Worth Spreading*, www.ted.com/. Accessed 21 Feb 2018.
7. Gallo, Carmine. *Talk Like TED: The 9 Public-Speaking Secrets of the World's Top Minds.* New York: St. Martins Press, 2014.
8. Cornish, David, and Dianne Dukette. *The Essential 20: Twenty Components of an Excellent Health Care Team.* Pittsburgh, PA: RoseDog Books, 2009.

Chapter 2

1. "BBC World Service | Learning English | Moving Words." *BBC News*, BBC, www.bbc.co.uk/worldservice/learningenglish/movingwords/ shortlist/ mandela.shtml. Accessed 21 Feb 2018.
2. The Daily Conversation. "Mitt Romney's "47 Percent' Comments." *YouTube*, YouTube, 18 Sept 2012, www.youtube.com/watch?v=M2gv Y2wqI7M. Accessed 21 Feb 2018.
3. Noonan, Peggy. *On Speaking Well: How to Give a Speech with Style, Substance, and Clarity*. HarperCollins, 1998.
4. Heifetz, Ronald Abadian, and Martin Linsky. *Leadership on the Line: Staying Alive through the Dangers of Leading*. Boston: Harvard Business Review Press, 2002.

Chapter 3

1. King, Stephen. *On Writing: A Memoir of the Craft*. Scribner, 2000, p. 57.
2. Lehrman, Robert A. *The Political Speechwriter's Companion: A Guide for Writers and Speakers*. CQ Press, 2009.
3. The U.S. Department of Housing and Urban Development, Office of Community Planning and Development. *The 2017 Annual Homeless Assessment Report (AHAR) to Congress*. December 2017. https://www. hudexchange.info/resources/documents/2017-AHAR-Part-1.pdf. Accessed 9 Mar 2018.
4. Cornish, David, and Dianne Dukette. *The Essential 20: Twenty Components of an Excellent Health Care Team*. Pittsburgh, PA: RoseDog Books, 2009.
5. "Cancer Stat Facts: Cancer of Any Site." *Surveillance, Epidemiology, and End Results Program*, National Cancer Institute, 2014, seer.cancer.gov/ statfacts/html/all.html. Accessed 21 Feb 2018.
6. United Nations High Commissioner for Refugees. "UNHCR viewpoint: 'Refugee' or 'migrant'—Which is right?" *UNHCR*, 11 July 2016, www. unhcr.org/en-us/news/latest/2016/7/55df0e556/unhcr-viewpoint- refugee-migrant-right.html. Accessed 21 Feb 2018.

Chapter 4

1. *The Internet Classics Archive | Rhetoric by Aristotle*, MIT, classics.mit. edu/Aristotle/rhetoric.html. Accessed 21 Feb 2018.
2. Kolbert, Elizabeth. "Why Facts Don't Change Our Minds." *New Yorker*, 27 Feb 2017, www.newyorker.com/magazine/2017/02/27/why-facts-dont-change-our-minds. Accessed 21 Feb 2018.
3. Heath, Chip, and Dan Heath. *Made to Stick: Why Some Ideas Survive and Others Die*. New York: Random House, 2007.
4. Zak, Paul J. "Why Your Brain Loves Good Storytelling." *Harvard Business Review*, 28 Oct. 2014, hbr.org/2014/10/why-your-brain-loves-good-storytelling. Accessed 21 Feb 2018.
5. Simmons, Annette. *Whoever Tells the Best Story Wins: How to Use Your Own Stories to Communicate with Power and Impact*. AMACOM, 2015.
6. Ganz, Marshall. "Public Narrative, Collective Action, and Power." *Digital Access to Scholarship at Harvard*, 2011, nrs.harvard.edu/urn-3:HUL.InstRepos:29314925. Accessed 21 Feb 2018.
7. "The Art and Craft of Storytelling." *The Moth*, www.themoth.org. Accessed 21 Feb 2018.
8. Ganz, Marshall. "Public Narrative, Collective Action, and Power." *Digital Access to Scholarship at Harvard*, 2011, nrs.harvard.edu/urn-3:HUL.InstRepos:29314925. Accessed 21 Feb 2018.
9. Hampes, William P. "Relation between Humor and Empathic Concern." *Psychological Reports*, vol. 88, no. 1, Feb. 2001, pp. 241–244, doi:10.2466/pr0.2001.88.1.241.
10. "GeorgeJesselQuotes." *BrainyQuote*, Xplore, www.brainyquote.com/citation/quotes/george_jessel_177118. Accessed 21 Feb 2018.

Chapter 5

1. Michelangelo Quotes. (n.d.). BrainyQuote.com. Retrieved 20 Jan 2018, from BrainyQuote.com: www.brainyquote.com/quotes/michelangelo_386296.
2. Noonan, Peggy. *On Speaking Well: How to Give a Speech with Style, Substance, and Clarity*. HarperCollins, 1998.

Chapter 6

1. Strongman, K. T., and B. G. Champness. "Dominance Hierarchies and Conflict in Eye Contact." *Acta Psychologica*, vol. 28, 1968, pp. 376–386., doi:10.1016/0001-6918(68)90026-7.

2. Spector, Nicole. "Smiling Can Trick Your Brain into Happiness—and Boost Your Health." *NBCNews.com*, NBC Universal News Group, 9 Jan 2018, www.nbcnews.com/better/health/smiling-can-trick-your-brain-happiness-boost-your-health-ncna822591. Accessed 21 Feb 2018.

3. Laukka, Petri, et al. "In a Nervous Voice: Acoustic Analysis and Perception of Anxiety in Social Phobics' Speech." *Journal of Nonverbal Behavior*, vol. 32, no. 4, 18 July 2008, pp. 195–214, doi:10.1007/s10919-008-0055-9.

4. Kraus, Michael W. "Voice-Only Communication Enhances Empathic Accuracy." *American Psychologist*, vol. 72, no. 7, 2017, pp. 644–654. Accessed 21 Feb 2018.

5. Mayhew, William J., et al. "Voice Pitch and the Labor Market Success of Male Chief Executive Officers." *Evolution and Human Behavior*, vol. 34, no. 4, July 2013. Accessed 21 Feb 2018.

6. Klofstad, Casey A., et al. "Sounds Like a Winner: Voice Pitch Influences Perception of Leadership Capacity in Both Men and Women." *Proceedings of the Royal Society of London B: Biological Sciences*, The Royal Society, 14 Mar. 2012, rspb.royalsocietypublishing.org/content/279/1738/2698.article-info. Accessed 21 Feb 2018.

7. Gardner, Bill. "From 'shrill' housewife to Downing Street: the changing voice of Margaret Thatcher." 25 Nov 2014. https://www.telegraph.co.uk/news/politics/11251919/From-shrill-housewife-to-Downing-Street-the-changing-voice-of-Margaret-Thatcher.html. Accessed 5 May 2018.

8. Finder, Robert L. Jr. *The Financial Professional's Guide to Communication: How to Strengthen Client Relationships and Build New Ones*. 1st ed., Pearson FT Press, 2012.

9. Gonçalves, Gláucia Renate. "Some Crucial Elements of Learning Ecologies of Linguistic Contagion." *New Challenges in Language and Literature*, by Tim Murphey, FALE/UFMG, 2009, pp. 129–147.

10. Dunn, Thom. "What Is 'Vocal Fry,' and Why Doesn't Anyone Care When Men Talk like That?" *Upworthy*, 28 July 2015, www.upworthy.com/what-is-vocal-fry-and-why-doesnt-anyone-care-when-men-talk-like-that. Accessed 21 Feb 2018. See also Glass, Ira, et al., "If You Don't Have Anything Nice to Say, SAY IT IN ALL CAPS." *This American Life*, 23 Jan 2015, www.thisamericanlife.org/radio-archives/episode/545/if-

you-dont-have-anything-nice-to-say-say-it-in-all-caps?act=2#play. Accessed 21 Feb 2018.

11. Anderson, Rindy C., et al. "Vocal Fry May Undermine the Success of Young Women in the Labor Market." *PLOS ONE*, Public Library of Science, 28 May 2014, journals.plos.org/plosone/article?id=10.1371 %2Fjournal.pone.0097506. Accessed 21 Feb 2018.

Chapter 7

1. Croston, Glenn. "The Thing We Fear More Than Death." *Psychology Today*, Sussex Publishers, 29 Nov 2012, www.psychologytoday.com/blog/ the-real-story-risk/201211/the-thing-we-fear-more-death. Accessed 21 Feb 2018.

2. Winch, Guy. "10 Surprising Facts About Rejection." *Psychology Today*, Sussex Publishers, 3 July 2013, www.psychologytoday.com/blog/the-squeaky-wheel/201307/10-surprising-facts-about-rejection. Accessed 21 Feb 2018.

3. DiSalvo, David. "Chew Yourself a Better Brain." *Forbes*, 8 Mar 2012, https://www. forbes.com/sites/daviddisalvo/2012/03/08/chew-yourself-a-better-brain/#77afddaa4dd6. Accessed 28 Apr 2018.

4. Do not perform this exercise if you have a medical condition that would prevent you from doing it safely or if your physician has advised you against such activity.

5. Kay, Katty, and Claire Shipman. *The Confidence Code: The Science and Art of Self-Assurance—What Women Should Know.* HarperCollins, 2014.

6. Creswell, J. D., et al. "Affirmation of Personal Values Buffers Neuroendocrine and Psychological Stress Responses." *Psychological Science*, vol. 16, no. 11, 16 Nov 2005, pp. 846–851.

Chapter 9

1. *Up in the Air*. Dir., Jason Reitman. Perf., George Clooney, Vera Farmiga, and Anna Kendrick. Paramount Pictures, 2009. DVD.

2. McAlone, Nathan. "These 5 Harvard Business School students built an app to help you sound more confident when you speak." 12 May 2016.

www.businessinsider.com/ummo-app-tracks-your-speech-2016-5. Accessed 28 Apr 2018.

3. "Myo Gesture Control Armband." *Myo Gesture Control Armband | Wearable Technology by Thalmic Labs*, www.myo.com/. Accessed 21 Feb 2018.

4. Duarte, Nancy. *slide:ology: The Art and Science of Creating Great Presentations*. O'Reilly Media, 2008.

5. Reynolds, Garr. *Simple Ideas on Presentation Design and Delivery*. New Riders, 2nd edition, 2011.

6. Kawasaki, Guy. *The Art of the Start 2.0: The Time-Tested, Battle-Hardened Guide for Anyone Starting Anything*. Portfolio, 2015.

7. superapple4ever. "Steve Jobs Introducing the iPhone At MacWorld 2007." *YouTube*, 2 Dec 2010, www.youtube.com/watch?v=x7qPAY9JqE4. Accessed 21 Feb 2018.

8. Tufte, Edward. "PowerPoint Does Rocket Science—and Better Techniques for Technical Reports." *Edward Tufte Forum*, www.edwardtufte.com/bboard/q-and-a-fetch-msg?msg_id=0001yB. Accessed 21 Feb 2018.

9. "Tony Robbins Live on Stage as a Humagram." *ARHT Media*, ARHT Media Inc., 20 June 2015, www.arhtmedia.com/blog/tony-robbins-live-on-stage-as-a-humagram/. Accessed 21 Feb 2018.

Chapter 11

1. Courville, Roger. *The Virtual Presenter's Handbook*. CreateSpace Independent Publishing Platform, 2009.

2. Nishiyama, Kazuo. *Doing Business with Japan: Successful Strategies for Intercultural Communication*. Latitude 20, 2000.

3. Woolstenhulme, Martin. "Mark Zuckerberg Speaks Chinese (English translation)." *YouTube*, 23 Oct 2014, https://www.youtube.com/watch?v=8Xpdhbh_2Rc . Accessed 17 June 2018.

Chapter 12

1. Hewlett, Sylvia Ann. *Executive Presence: The Missing Link between Merit and Success*. HarperBusiness, 2014.

2. Cialdini, Robert B. *Influence: The Psychology of Persuasion, Revised Edition*. Harper Business, 2006.
3. Hedges, Kristi. *The Power of Presence: Unlock Your Potential to Influence and Engage Others*. AMACOM, 2017.

Chapter 13

1. Ganz, Marshall. "Public Narrative, Collective Action, and Power." *Digital Access to Scholarship at Harvard*, 2011, nrs.harvard.edu/urn-3:HUL.InstRepos:29314925. Accessed 21 Feb 2018.
2. "Dalai Lama Quotes." *BrainyQuote*, Xplore, www.brainyquote.com/quotes/dalai_lama_393080. Accessed 21 Feb 2018.
3. Whitman, Gordon. *Stand Up! How to Get Involved, Speak Out, and Win in a World on Fire*. Berrett-Koehler Publishers, 2018.

Index